Making My Mark

Making My Mark is the personal memoir of Marvin Arrington's rise from humble beginnings to political prominence. He is a man who made his mark.

—Tom Wolfe, author

To read Marvin Arrington's autobiography is to be reminded of how someone in this country, combining strength of mind and resilience of character, could make of great obstacles only small hindrances and could shape adversity into possibility. As president of Emory University, Mr. Arrington's alma mater, I hope this book serves as a light of hope to all who read it. This is the story of a splendid American.

—William M. Chace, past president, Emory University

Atlanta's story is a tapestry of many threads and voices that have helped to weave the city's rich, vivid history. Marvin Arrington tells his story from his heart and it is a valued contribution to a city he dearly loves.

—Mayor Shirley Franklin, city of Atlanta

Making My Mark is a highly readable and inspiring account of Marvin Arrington's remarkable journey and the obstacles he overcame to achieve his place of success and accomplishment. On the last page of the book, Marvin hopes that a lot of young people will look at his life and see themselves. They will.

— Donald R. Keough

Marvin Arrington has written a story that epitomizes the American dream. *Making My Mark* is about overcoming adversity in a South that was a different place than it is now. Marvin overcame every obstacle in order to become one of the premier lawyers of our time and a leader in the field of civil rights. The South is different today because of a handful of people like Marvin Arrington. I am pleased that Marvin has taken the time and effort to share with all of us his struggle. I am honored to call him my friend.

—Roy E. Barnes, former governor of Georgia

Marvin Arrington has afforded us the opportunity to share the arduous road traveled by African Americans in pursuit of political involvement. The candor and sometimes stark reflections inform people of just how difficult that road can be. He shows by his own example that, we have come far. But his exhortation to others clearly demonstrates the need to be vigilant now more that ever. It can be well said that Marvin Arrington did the best that he could with what he had.

—L. Douglas Wilder, former governor of Virginia

Reading Making My Mark I was not surprised that Marvin was one of the first two African-Americans to graduate from the prestigious Emory Law School. As a student of the 60s, Marvin was part of the generation that blazed America's conscience on civil rights through the taunts of black power and the courage of sit-ins. Marvin literally stared the Klan in the face. Although he never forgot the insults they hurled at him, Marvin developed the capacity to love his enemies as he matured. He learned to make his mark. I strongly suspect that the boys around Ashby and Simpson Streets in northwest Atlanta taught Marvin a few things that also gave him the courage and determination to make his mark.

—Andrew Young, former US ambassador

Marvin Arrington's autobiography is the story of an African American who came out of an impoverished, abusive environment to become a leading political force in Atlanta politics.

Marvin's success is noteworthy and worth the telling: It is a *must* for those who struggle against the odds and succeed; it's a *must* for those who seek a more complete understanding of how the civil rights revolution impacted the poor; it's a *must* for those black intellectuals who claim to represent the black intelligentsia; and it's a *must* for those at the top who do not yet understand how their policies, practices, and attitudes affect the poor and working class people of America.

Marvin's experiences are inspirational because of his *guts*, *drive*, and *unyielding determination* to *succeed*!

—Clarence Cooper, US District Court judge,
North District of Georgia

In reading *Making My Mark*, I couldn't help but reflect on the parallels of the paths traveled by Marvin and me. And while my road lead me to continue the struggle that was started by Jackie Robinson, and Marvin's road lead him to be a warrior in the political and civil rights struggles of Atlanta, neither of us would have been successful if we had not developed the courage to make our marks. Without that courage, both of us could easily have been the victims of a caste system among our own people. Without the courage and determination to make our marks it's doubtful either of us would have risen above humble backgrounds in segregated Southern cities. *Making My Mark* is a story about courage and character. It's a story about a fight for dignity and integrity. It's a story about a common-sense approach to good government. *Making My Mark* is a story about a real winner—Marvin Arrington.

Henry "Hank" Aaron

This book is a fascinating and rewarding look into an important period of Atlanta's history as well as into the mind of Marvin Arrington. In this book, Marvin has conveyed the essence of his being—complex yet simple, confident yet often insecure, calm yet sometimes angry. It is a story of how a loving mother, good role models, passion, and hard work enabled a young black man from humble roots to grow into a respected lawyer and community leader with many friends—poor and rich, black and white, uppercrust and everyday. The autobiography of Marvin Arrington is an interesting read.

—President Jimmy Carter

Marvin Arrington's *Making My Mark* is especially enjoyable and meaningful to those of us who have known and admired Marvin as a public servant, lawyer, civic leader, judge, and friend because it gives perspective to his outstanding record of leadership.

Marvin captures the unfairness and discrimination of the past, the remarkable—but not yet complete—changes for the better, and different but difficult obstacles faced by our younger generation. His message is both relevant and compelling to our present and our future. It comes from a judge who has himself faced and overcome many obstacles and who sees everyday the devastation to individuals and society caused by lack of motivation, lack of education, and lack of skills and self-confidence, particularly in an environment of drugs and senseless violence.

Marvin Arrington's life story is, however, a message of hope, courage, determination, persistence, rising above expectations, and dedicated service to others. He shows us—by his own experience—that if you 'make your mark,' it makes you stronger, smarter, and more determined to succeed.

Making My Mark is an inspirational message to us all. For our young people, it can be life changing.

—Honorable Sam Nunn, former US senator

Making My Mark is both a delightful and important work. For those of us who are African American and whose ages range from fifty to the sixty, Marvin chronicles familiar circumstances—segregated public places, limited educational and work opportunities, and outright discrimination—all in a very informative narrative. But, regardless of one's background, the book is a truly inspirational read. The details of how one courageous, tenacious, talented, and wise individual overcame incredible adversity to become one of Atlanta's most successful lawyers and powerful public figures comes alive in the book's pages. From being relegated to Atlanta's "colored park" to being subjected to a bruising mayoral campaign based on scandalous and false allegations, Marvin Arrington always succeeded. A remarkable story of perseverance, street smarts, political savvy, good judgment, and unfailing success unfolds in this book.

This book is also a paean to Marvin Arrington's love of Atlanta. Friends, colleagues, classmates, places, and events are lovingly and poignantly described. And, perhaps most importantly, the book offers a glimpse of how one can achieve a life fulfilled. In the end, it is Marvin Arrington's complete dedication to public service and his city that allows him, after many tumultuous years, to look back on his life and write with such satisfaction and fulfillment.

—Larry D. Thompson, Sr., vice president,
general counsel and secretary of Pepsico

Making My Mark tells the story of a remarkable Emory alumnus—one of the first two African Americans to enroll in Emory Law School, the first black administrator at Emory, a long-serving trustee and advisor to Emory presidents, parent and uncle of Emory law a alumni, and public servant extraordinaire. Marvin Arrington's inspiring story is a fascinating account, one that is rich with adventure and accomplishment.

—James W. Wagner, president, Emory University

Making My Mark

The Story of a Man Who Wouldn't Stay in His Place

Marvin S. Arrington, Sr.

Mercer University Press
Macon, Georgia

MUP/H751
ISBN 978-0-88146-098-8

© Marvin S. Arrington Sr. 2008

Published by Mercer University Press
1400 Coleman Avenue
Macon, Georgia 31207
All rights reserved

First Edition - 5th printing

Books published by Mercer University Press are printed on acid free paper that
meets the requirements of American National Standard for Information
Sciences—Permanence of Paper for Printed Library Materials.

meets the requirements of American National Standard for Information

Library of Congress Cataloging-in-Publication Data

Arrington, Marvin S.
Making my mark : the story of a man who wouldn't stay in his place /
Marvin S. Arrington, Sr.
p. cm.
Includes index.
ISBN-13: 978-0-88146-098-8 (hardback : alk. paper)
ISBN-10: 0-88146-098-2
1. Lawyers—Georgia—Biography. 2. Judges—Georgia—Biography. I. Title.
KF373.A72A3 2008
340.092—dc22
[B]
2008006230

Dedication

"No man is an island," wrote John Donne. His words remind me that so many individuals have poured into my life. There were the brave warriors of public education, the teachers who saw something special in me and inspired in me a quest for learning. There was the genius of L. S. Epps, my college football coach, who taught me fair play and that winning comes from giving all I have no matter how difficult the challenge. There are my brothers and sisters and their children, who are a testament to the pursuit of higher education and a love for the law, reflected in the fact that two of my siblings, both of my children, and a niece and nephew all earned law degrees. I celebrate them all in this book.

However, I dedicate this documentation of my life's journey to the three women who nurtured and sustained me over the years, my two children, and three grandchildren

To Maggie Ruth Arrington, my mother, I give my undying love and affection for always being there for me. Your spirit and strength continuously echoed to me, "Don't give up! Hang in there!" You were not only my mother but also my friend, my ally, and my rock.

To Myrtle Jones, the perfect mother-in-law, I am grateful you challenged my children to be all that they could be and for all the help that you gave to their rearing.

To Marilyn Jones Arrington, my wife of thirty-one years, you gave me the greatest gift of all—my two wonderful children, Marvin S. Arrington, Jr., and Michelle Dubois Arrington. Thank you for being an excellent mother, for you took the lead in nurturing and developing two fine young people of whom we are both extremely proud.

I want this book to be a reminder of what I have learned on my journey so that you, Marvin, Michelle, Kennedy, Kendall, and Madison will share in this legacy and take up the reigns of leadership to make Atlanta and the world a better place in which to live.

> *Children are the world's most valuable resources and its best hope for the future.*
>
> —John F. Kennedy

God's blessings I pray will always be upon you.

Contents

Foreword

I became acquainted with Marvin Arrington some thirty-five years ago. I noticed something special about him and the way he interacted with others as a frequent customer at my parents' Westside Atlanta restaurant. In particular, I observed his ability to advocate on the behalf of others, his willingness to provide access regardless of status, and his knack for using his profession to build bridges across the Atlanta social strata.

Upon discovering my interest in becoming an attorney, he quickly transitioned from role model to active mentor. In the early years, he encouraged me by inviting me to his law firm to meet other lawyers, arranging summer internships with the city of Atlanta, completing law school recommendations, traveling to my law school to provide a keynote address, and hiring me as a summer law clerk at his firm. After law school, he continued to provide support and counsel as I served in numerous capacities—as in-house counsel for one of Atlanta's largest corporations, a managing director of the Atlanta committee for the Olympic Games, associate judge of the Fulton County Juvenile Court, and chief senior assistant district attorney. Marvin Arrington wasn't just an inspiration to an ambitious teenager; he has profoundly affected his community.

Marvin Arrington's life and the history of the city of Atlanta have been inextricably linked for the last six decades. In fact, almost everyone who played a role in shaping Atlanta as it transitioned from a provincial, segregated town into an international city has encountered Atlanta's favorite son. He has functioned in numerous positions:

- In the 50s, he rejected segregationist efforts to encourage low self-esteem, dehumanization, and a low appreciation of education.

- In the 60s, he participated in the civil rights struggles and broke down barriers at Emory, Atlanta's most prestigious university.
- In the 70s, he joined Atlanta's political establishment and formed one of Atlanta's first integrated law firms.
- In the 80s, he became president of the Atlanta City Council; his law practice expanded to represent some of Atlanta's major businesses.
- In the 90s, he served as city council president while the city of Atlanta experienced unprecedented international investment and worldwide recognition as the host of the 1996 Olympics.
- After 2000, he transitioned from the legislative branch to the judicial branch while continuing to serve his community as a senior statesman.

Unlike many of his contemporaries, Marvin Arrington did not inherit a tradition of prominence and position. It was by his own hard work, intelligence, and tenacity that he has made a name for himself. Daily he defied the odds and overcame barriers of race, class, privilege, and color prejudice. His accomplishments have been the result of his affirmation of his God-given potential.

Marvin Arrington has established himself as one of Atlanta's most prominent lawyer-lawmakers. He has used his skills in public service as a government poverty rights attorney, city legislator, and superior court judge. As private counsel, he has represented individuals of all walks in life in both criminal and civil matters. In addition, he has represented small business owners as well as *Fortune* 500 corporations. He now serves on the top-tier trial court where he dispenses justice without the fear of making unpopular decisions where justice so demands.

Without a doubt, no other African-American attorney has had an equally profound effect on the careers of so many of Atlanta's African-American attorneys and judges. Inevitably, a relationship leads back to Marvin Arrington. On the other hand, he has served the greater legal community by providing training and mentorship for the first wave of African-American attorneys who integrated major and mid-sized law firms, corporations, and the judiciary; he has provided a model of an integrated law firm; and, as a student and faculty member, he has championed diversity at Emory University.

His brilliance has often been overshadowed by his humility and "groundedness." He has endeared himself to his fellow citizens because he is approachable, accessible, and empathetic. In addition, he remains a beacon of loyalty, fairness, generosity, and good humor. In other words, in a time when so many young people are in need of direction, Marvin Arrington's life is an excellent source of inspiration.

David Getachew-Smith, Sr.
Yale University '76
London School of Economics
Harvard Law School '80

Grady Baby. This 1945 photo of Marvin
Arrington is displayed in the bby of
Grady Memorial Hospital (Atlanta) as a
"Grady baby."

(Left to right) Marvin Arrington with his
mother Maggie Arrington and sisters
Audrey Arrington and Cynthia Arrington
(now Cynthia Arrington Wright), 1949.

Carter Elementary School Band. Marvin Arrington, age nine, on bass drum.

Marvin Arrington, age ten, at English Avenue Elementary School.

Washington Park Tennis Center Youth Tennis Players (left to right) Horace Reid, Marvin Arrington, and Willie Whited, 1984.

On the campus of Howard University School of Law, 1965.

Graduation day, Emory University School of Law, 1967.

The Arrington family (left to right): Marilyn, Marvin Junior, Michelle, and Marvin Senior. Photo by Gittings Southeastern, Inc., 1989.

Marvin Arrington with his mother Maggie, his mentor and inspiration, 1975.

Grandchildren (left to right) Kendall, Madison, and Kennedy, 2006.

The Arrington family of lawyers (pictured left to right) Marvin Jr., Audrey, Jill, Marvin Sr., Michelle, Joseph, Joseph II, 2004. Photo by Alex Jones.

Lifelong friends and Kappa Alpha Psi Fraternity brothers (left to right) Judge Marvin Arrington, attorney James L. Hudson, and Dr. Thomas J. Washington III, 1996.

Marvin Arrington, Dr. Hamilton Holmes, who integrated the University of Georgia, and Marilyn Holmes, 1993.

A gathering of current and former Atlanta City Council presidents at the induction of Hank Aaron into the Baseball Hall of Fame in Cooperstown NY (left to right): city council president Marvin Arrington, Coca Cola executive Carl Ware, Senator Wyche Fowler, and Mayor Maynard Jackson, 1982.

Co-chairs of the 1999 Southwest Community Hospital Capital Campaign: Ambassador Andrew Young and Marvin Arrington. Photo by Wayne Parham.

Announcement of funding for a City of Atlanta CETA program. City council president Marvin Arrington, and President George H. W. Bush, together with business leaders, 1993. Photo by Bud Smith.

1997 mayoral campaign.

Former Atlanta Board of Education chair Preston Williams, honored guest
Desmond Tutu, and Clark University trustee Marvin Arrington at a reception at
Clark Atlanta University, 1992.

Rosa Parks and city council president Marvin Arrington at a reception at Atlanta City Hall. Photo by Susan J. Ross, 1991.

Law day reception at Emory University, trustee and alumnus Marvin Arrington with author Tom Wolfe, 1998.

Hank Aaron receiving honorary doctorate degree at Emory University Commencement with Emory University Trustee Marvin Arrington, 1995.

Swearing in of Larry Thompson as deputy attorney general of the United States of America, 2001.

Marvin Arrington and Ben Johnson, former dean of Emory University School of Law. Dean Johnson admitted Judge Marvin Arrington and US District Court Judge Clarence Cooper to Emory Law. Picture taken at a reception in honor of Ben Johnson receiving the Community Service Award from Georgia State University, 1994.

Marvin Arrington with his mentor and former law partner, Donald L. Hollowell, noted civil rights attorney, whose clients included Dr. Martin Luther King, Jr.

A gathering of former law partners and associates (left to right): Jay Strongwater, Richard Rubin, Judge Marvin Arrington, Elizabeth "Betsy" Edelman, Judge John "Jack" Goger, David Krischer, David Walbert, 2001.

Senior partner Arrington and Hollowell, 1998. Photo by Kay Hinton.

Recipient of Justice Robert Benham's Community Service Award with then Georgia State Bar President Linda Klein and Chief Justice Robert Benham, 1998.

Chapter 1

The Fire This Time

Friday, March 11, 2005

That, obviously, is not where my story begins, but it clearly was one of those pivotal moments in which I was brought face-to-face with everything I feared; that this day would be the end of my story, that I might die and never again see my children or other people in my life who are dear to me.

It was a day of sheer terror. People across the nation watched on their televisions as the ordeal unfolded. Pandemonium, fear, confusion, chaos ruled as a gunman wreaked havoc on the Fulton County Courthouse in downtown Atlanta. His brazen attack left me and other captives feeling vulnerable and powerless. It brought the city to its knees and shattered our sense of security.

As a Fulton County Superior Court judge who was on the bench that morning, I was one of the many people trapped by this young man's rampage. Before it ended many hours later, the tragedy would leave one of my fellow jurists dead, along with a court reporter, a sheriff's deputy, and a federal immigration agent.

Being on lockdown in my office, with little or no information while this deadly tragedy played out, must have been what it's like to be in the middle of a palace coup. It began for us when, without warning, the sheriff's deputy who served as the bailiff for my courtroom, rushed us from the courtroom and into my office. It was a little past nine in the morning. All he said was that Judge (Rowland)

Barnes had been shot in his courtroom; we were to stay put and not open the door for anybody—except him. He would knock three times when he returned so we would know it was safe to open the door.

Several agonizing hours later, I learned that Judge Barnes had been assassinated on the bench by a defendant who was on trial at the time. The killer was a young black man who managed to overpower a deputy, get her gun, and enter the judge's courtroom through his chambers. The young man shot Judge Barnes at point-blank range. The judge's back was to the door, so he likely never knew what happened. The young man shot the court reporter, too, before fleeing the building, where he then shot and killed a deputy who was trying to keep him from escaping the scene. While on the run, he also gunned down a federal immigration officer.

But on that frightening Friday morning, all we (myself, the court reporter, secretaries, lawyers, and others holed up in my office) knew was that all Hell had broken loose and one among us—a man whose job it was to sit in judgment of others, as I did every day—had been executed by one whose freedom the judge had balanced in his hands. It was a jurist's worst nightmare come true. Those were excruciating hours of waiting for news and the "all-clear." Information came slowly, in torturous bits and pieces as the drama unfolded and we continued to wait. A killer was on the loose, but no one was sure whether there might be others—or if he had left the courthouse. Was he hiding? Were there others on his execution list? What were the sheriff's deputies and the police doing? Was this an act of terrorism? Was the FBI involved yet?

If the killer had managed to get out of the building, how had he done it? Wasn't this one of the most secure buildings in all of Atlanta, especially after the terrorist attacks of September 11, 2001?

Morning dragged into afternoon, then late afternoon. The suspense of having no answers was taking its toll. Then more news: The killer *had* managed to escape the courthouse. It was believed that he was driving around the northern sections of Atlanta in a series of hijacked cars. It would be early the next day—long after they'd finally released us to go home—that the killer would give himself up, peacefully, and leave us to figure out how so many things had gone so terribly wrong.

For me, that wasn't the only question. Moments like those make one question one's whole life; how had I come to be in that position? Was God trying to get my attention? Was I doing what I should be doing with my life? Was being a judge the kind of public service to which I wanted to devote the rest of my working life? I'd spent nearly thirty years in service to the people of Atlanta as a member of the old board of aldermen and as a city council member and president before moving to the bench. Or, was this experience just one more of the "tough lessons" of my hardscrabble life?

I had been appointed to the superior court bench by then-governor Roy Barnes after a long career practicing law and serving in city government. Frankly, I'd never expected to wind up on the bench after spending most of my adult life in courtrooms, mostly as a defense attorney. I had assumed that I would cap my career of public service in a different capacity: mayor of Atlanta. It seemed to me that the twists, turns, and experiences of my life pointed me in that direction. Others in the city shared that belief, and many people over the years had encouraged me to seek that office. But I had declined for one reason or another, particularly when my two children were still being educated. But in 1997, I decided it was time, and I threw my hat into the ring against Bill Campbell.

I was beaten, but I use the word "beaten" loosely here. I was the victim of a vicious campaign by many people who tried to ruin me personally as well as politically. Among other things, they tried to paint me as a Republican (a label that was the kiss of death in the black community at that time) and as a crook who had taken money from people wanting to do business with the city. These malicious tactics were carried out through innuendo, rumors, and scurrilous mass mailings. And, to be more frank than is politically correct, I believe I was also a victim of a *sub rosa* phenomenon that still plagues portions of our society (and even the city of Atlanta, a place several national publications anointed as "The Black Mecca"): my complexion was too dark for the comfort of too many people, especially when a "black" option was available that was much less so.

The sad irony in all of this is that those who tried to label me a crook during that election have run up more criminal indictments than any other Atlanta mayoral administration in anybody's memory, perhaps in history. Even former mayor Bill Campbell has been convicted of three counts of tax evasion and sentenced to thirty months in prison and a $6,000 fine.

For me, however, the parade of indictments, guilty pleas, and convictions of members of his administration and close associates came too late to aid my mayoral ambitions. I would like to think that, maybe, if more of the truth had been known at the time, I might have reached what I had come to believe was the destiny of this black boy, this son of Atlanta. But it is likely too late for me now. Yet the pain of it still sticks in my craw. I am a product of this city. I paid my dues, served Atlanta well, and deserved better than I got from my opponent and from many of my fellow citizens. But that pain and disappointment are illustrative of my life. I have always gained strength, new insights, and a deeper hunger to succeed whenever life has knocked me down.

My purpose here is to shed light on the life I've lived and, perhaps, inspire others to keep the faith, and just keep on pushing, no matter how bleak things seem. My beginnings were humble, but I have been blessed. I have been able to serve others, and through that service, I have lived richly—even when my pockets were empty.

Atlanta has not always seemed to love me, but I have always loved her. And I am proud to be a native son of this irrepressible city of the Phoenix, which has endured countless hardships, near destruction, and the challenges of her own flaws and shortcomings. Atlanta has not merely held its own among this country's most promising cities; she has grown and prospered at a rate that many of them envy. The city that birthed and raised me has knocked me down more than a few times, but it has also lifted me up. Like the city I love, I know how to rise from the ashes. That is what my life has been about. It has truly been a life worth living, and even as I move through the autumn of my years, I know that I am not finished rising yet. For my life and the life of this city are interwoven into a tapestry of destiny that has always given me purpose and hope, even though I might not have understood that clearly every step of the way.

But more about that later. It's time I went back to the beginning. It helps to understand how I became the man I am.

Chapter 2

A Tradition of Family

My life began not unlike that of millions of other African Americans. In the early 1800s, my great-great-great-grandparents, Moses and Hattie Hitchcock, were brought as slaves from Virginia to Baldwin County, Georgia. They had six sons (Glasco, Sam, Hiram, Mose, Flay, and Dennard) and three daughters (Martha Ann, Alice, and Julia). All of Moses and Hattie's sons grew up to farm their own land, and the daughters married small landowners. The longtime presence of the Hitchcock family in Baldwin County was recognized in recent years when a street in Milledgeville was named after them.

Their oldest son, Glasco Hitchcock, although born into slavery, became a successful businessman with a small store and lived to be 106. Glasco and his wife, Polly, had seven children. Their son Sam was married five times and had eighteen children, including my maternal grandmother, Ida. Ida married Johnny Andrews ("Papa Jack," as we called him), and their children included my mother, Maggie Andrews.

Then the boll weevil made its steady march through Georgia, devastating the cotton-based economy county by county. Papa Jack left his family on the farm in Milledgeville in 1920 and headed to Atlanta in search of work. He lived with family in Atlanta, eventually getting a custodial job at the *Atlanta Journal*, and then at an apartment building across the street from Piedmont Park. Although his financial situation was still tenuous, Papa Jack couldn't stand to be away from his family very long, so he moved them to the city. My mother and her siblings, raised in rural Georgia, were awed by what they saw in Atlanta. They'd never seen a building as large as the railroad terminal and were mesmerized by the elevator in the building at 1206 Peachtree Street where Papa Jack found his next job as janitor.

As a child, my mother was fortunate in the timing of the family's move to Atlanta. The NAACP in 1921 succeeded in a tremendous voter registration drive, leading to a successful bond referendum to fund the construction of five new schools for African-American children. These schools replaced run-down nineteenth-century wooden school buildings, which had been filled to overflowing in double shifts as families sought education for their children. Mother was among the first students to attend Edwin P. Johnson School, on the corner of Fulton and Martin streets in the Summerhill neighborhood.

Times were difficult for the family, but they never went hungry, thanks to the meals Papa Jack brought home from the dining room in the Piedmont Apartment building. When Mother was in the fourth grade, Papa Jack moved the family to the Pittsburgh section of the city, where she went to William H. Crogman School, also recently constructed. She completed the sixth grade there in 1927. She attended Booker T. Washington High School, Atlanta's first high school for black students, through the twelfth grade. But she left school to marry my father before she graduated.

My paternal grandfather, Idus Arrington, was from Chipley, Georgia (now known as Pine Mountain), and the story told by my mother and others is that my grandfather got into a Saturday-night brawl and killed a man in self-defense. Even so, he fled to Atlanta and began working for a white family who had the name Arrington. He adopted that name so that he could hide his identity. My grandfather then moved on to Knoxville, Tennessee, and occasionally our family visited him. He was a laborer and was reputed to be a lady's man, but he always treated us with respect. I don't ever remember any of us being disciplined by him.

When Mother and Dad married on March 28, 1935, they settled in the Summerhill area, where my father worked hard and lived hard, hustling for a buck wherever he could find one.

My oldest brother, Joe, was born in 1937. He was followed by my sister, Yvonne, and then me. My younger sister, Ida Patricia, died soon after birth, but then my parents had two more children, Audrey LaRuth and Cynthia LaVerne. We were all born in Grady Hospital in downtown Atlanta. As testimony to my father's lifestyle, I also had a half-brother, Bobby George, Dad's son from another relationship.

At the time I was born in 1941, my father, George Arrington, drove a truck for the Bell Bomber company and worked in a drugstore. Known as "Bully" on the street, Dad did whatever it took to earn a buck, including selling moonshine and playing the numbers, a local lottery enterprise more commonly known as "the bug." People in our community often supplemented their incomes in a variety of creative—and illegal—ways, including this lottery. It's ironic now to see the state of Georgia running a lottery after throwing so many people in jail for doing the exact same thing.

We lived in apartment 227 in Grady Homes, and Dad always had an eye on moving up. He thought about moving to Detroit, to work in the newly desegregated automobile industry where he could have made a lot more money. But he hit big on the numbers when I was three years old, and he decided to become a property owner. He paid cash for a three-bedroom house at 883 Neal Street and opened a grocery store and butcher shop at 559 English Avenue.

My mother worked as a maid and focused her attention on making sure all of us found our seats every Sunday at Bethlehem Baptist Church in Summerhill, then later at Lindsay Street Baptist Church. At Lindsey Street Baptist, the Reverend H. M. Alexander built a Christian foundation in each of us—a foundation upon which we could grow for the rest of our lives.

During my formative years, the churches prepared the fields for the civil rights movement. Great leaders like Martin Luther King, Sr., at Ebenezer Baptist, William Holmes Borders at Wheat Street Baptist, Bishop Bearden at Big Bethel A. M. E., Homer McEwen at First Congregational, and Sam Williams at Providence Baptist, led voter registration drives and met with the mayor and others in an effort to knock down the barriers of discrimination. They were determined to make America "right" for theirs and all succeeding generations.

I was also greatly influenced in my childhood by Warren Cochrane at the Butler Street Y. M. C. A., where those of us whose mothers worked spent many after-school hours.

As a child, I saw Mr. Cochrane order two white policemen out of the Butler Street "Y" with a stern reprimand that if they came into the building again being disrespectful, he would call Police Chief Herbert Jenkins himself and ask that they be given a formal reprimand. That was the first time in my life that I ever saw a black man stand toe-to-toe with white police officers and talk them down.

Only later did I learn that Mr. Cochrane was one of the most powerful black non politicians in the city of Atlanta at the time. When Chief Jenkins hired Atlanta's first black police officers in 1948, they were not allowed to use the facilities at the police station. So Mr. Cochrane let them change into their uniforms in the basement of the "Y."

Later, when the chief assigned white police officers to work with black police officers, the white officers put in for sick leave. Within thirty days Jenkins was fed up with this tactic. He called a meeting and told officers that the next time he assigned white officers to work with black officers and the white officers put in for sick leave, he would fire them. It was that strong statement from the chief that forced integration in a way that made Atlanta's police department better.

In addition to his relationship with Chief Jenkins, Warren Cochrane had a great relationship with mayors William T. Hartsfield and Ivan Allen, Jr., and as far as I know, no one disrespected him. He had learned when and where to flex his muscles.

My teenage years were tough at home, and I spent much of my time on the street. My father and I didn't get along. He was a physical man who, when angered, never hesitated to hit me with whatever was within reach—a large clothes brush, a piece of chimney wood. I vowed then that if I ever became a father I would never abuse my children, and I kept that vow. Marvin, Jr., probably wasn't spanked more than two or three times in his childhood. He knew when I was serious. He could see it in my eyes, and he responded appropriately.

As a little boy, I feared my father more than I respected him. As a teenager, I just wanted to get away from him. I had come to understand that my father was a ladies' man—out of the house three or four nights a week. I am not aware that my mother ever questioned him about his activities, but the evidence couldn't be denied.

When my father invited his mother to move in with us without consulting Mama, the tension only increased. Mama took care of her mother-in-law every morning before catching the bus to work and every night when she came home.

When I was fourteen years old, my father was still enforcing his rules in our house with physical abuse. Finally, I refused to submit to any more beatings. One day when he was about to administer another beating for no apparent reason, I walked out. I got on the bus and moved in with my maternal grandmother in Lynwood Park, a couple of miles north of Oglethorpe College. There I lived for the first time with outdoor toilet facilities, a humbling experience for me that left one of those marks you carry inside for the rest of your life. In order to get to school from my grandmother's house, I had to get up before dawn, walk two miles to the bus stop on Peachtree Street, catch the Number 16 bus into downtown, and then transfer to the Dixie Hills bus that got me to school by 8:00 A.M. Mother wanted to restore peace, and she urged me to apologize to Dad. My feelings had not changed, but I was worn out by the commute, so I conceded and was allowed to come back home.

During my high school days I was something of a leader in my neighborhood and liked my tough reputation. In many cases, I had no choice but to be tough. I got off the school bus and was walking home from school one day when I heard a girl screaming for help from behind the bushes. I ran to investigate and found my own sister being attacked by two boys intent on raping her. Both of the boys tried to run, and I could only catch one of them. When I finished with him, he had to be taken to Grady Hospital. For a while, the doctors weren't sure he would make it.

The boy's older brother called later and said, "You're gonna live to regret that."

"Any time, any place, man," I said. "You tell me where to meet." He never challenged me.

Then the boy's mother complained to my parents that I had almost killed her son.

Dad replied, "He got what he deserves. Nobody has the right to physically attack one of my daughters like that." My father may have beaten me, but nobody outside the family was going to mess with us.

When the time came years later to start my own family, my goal was to maintain the closeness of the Arringtons without the fear and intimidation my brother, sisters, and I grew up with. But I was in no hurry to get married.

It was a law school paper—not a party or a blind date—that brought me together with Marilyn Jones, the woman who would later become my wife. I had to get a paper typed and didn't know anybody on the Emory campus who could help, so I drove over to Clark College and started asking around. Somebody told me about a young lady who was a typist. I looked up Marilyn Jones, and I think I offered her something like $5. She did a great job, but she wouldn't take any money. I asked her if I could take her to dinner for being so nice. I didn't tell her right off that I thought she was beautiful, and that, if she would go out with me I would consider myself two times a winner.

And, she didn't tell me she was going to bring one of her roommates along. The three of us arrived at Paschal's restaurant, and I had only twelve dollars in my pocket, so I decided to forego drinks and a meal for myself.

"I'm on a diet," I said, because if I had ordered, somebody would have been washing dishes.

Later, I asked Marilyn out again, and this time her roommate didn't chaperone us. We dated for about a year and a half, and I enjoyed getting to know her and her family. Marilyn had grown up in Rome, Georgia, where her father managed the local office of the Atlanta Life Insurance Company. Early in the civil rights movement, he had often posted bond for student protesters in Rome when no one else would.

Marilyn and I drifted apart after a while, and I moved on with my career. A few years later, she was teaching at Bass High School near Little Five Points, and we started dating again. I was practicing law and serving on the Atlanta Board of Aldermen. We married on May 17, 1971, and rented a place in Jade East Apartments on Collier Road.

After Marvin, Jr., was born, the family, professional, and political pressures just about wore me out. All the same, I practiced law full time and tried to fulfill my obligations as a father and a husband. I often took work home rather than stay late at the office. At least then I was near my family, even if I wasn't interacting as much as I might like. I would sit at the table to put together questions for *voir dire* and cross examinations or to practice my opening and closing arguments. Marilyn continued teaching in the Atlanta public schools, so neither of us spent as much time with Marvin in those early years as we wished. When he was a baby, I would drop him off at the nursery at Central Presbyterian Church in front of city hall, and Marilyn would pick him up in the afternoon. Looking back, I have to say that was a mistake. I was chasing the buck too hard in those early years. Our family would have been a lot better off if Marilyn had stayed home full time and I had worked less. After the IRS got through with her paycheck and we paid for childcare, we didn't earn that much more money anyway.

But I believe Marvin understood our love for him, as did his younger sister, Michelle. They both are now in their early adult years, and we are closer than ever. Marvin, Jr., joined my law firm and, once I retired, left the firm and set up his own practice. Michelle graduated from Howard University and, later, the law school at DePaul University.

Chapter 3

Discovering "My Place"

In the warm west Georgia twilight half a century ago, my father might have died a violent death in front of me and the rest of my family. Instead, I learned a lesson about white people, black people, and the South—a lesson that I hope none who follows behind me ever has to learn. I was eight years old that summer evening and we were driving back to Atlanta after a visit with relatives down in Chipley (now known as Pine Mountain). My older brother had seen a road stand selling peaches somewhere along the way, and he started pestering Dad to stop and buy some. Dad said he would stop when he found some that looked good, but he drove by several stands without even slowing. The sun had set, the sky was quickly fading from orange to red to gray, and Joe kept after Dad. Finally, Dad pulled over at the edge of some woods where some folks were just packing up their stand for the day. He bought a sack of peaches and was walking back to the car when three white men appeared from the woods.

"Hey, boy," one of the men said.

Dad didn't turn. He just kept walking toward the car.

"Boy, didn't you hear me talking to you?" the man said, and my father stopped and turned.

"What's the problem?" Dad asked.

"We got a car stuck back up in the woods and we need one more man to help us get it out."

Well, my father wasn't about to go back in the west Georgia woods with three white men in the 1950s, but he tried to be polite, if not obliging.

"I'm sorry," he said, "but I have my family with me here, and we're trying to get back home before it gets too late."

"Only take us a minute, boy," another of the men said, taking a step toward Dad.

Dad said, "You put your hand on me, somebody's gonna die right here. Now, I'm going to get in my car and we're going to continue to drive on our way. If you're stuck, I'm sorry, but that's your problem."

He got in the car, and we left because he believed something crazy was about to happen. While they never threatened us directly, my father just wasn't going to take a chance. The situation could have been completely innocent. Looking back, though, I think not. Dad taught me through his actions to be sensitive to what's going on around me.

Five years later the lesson was reinforced.

Despite what I had seen, I found it hard to believe white people would abuse black children, especially in our own neighborhood. Of course, I knew white people had it better than we did, and some of them were working hard to keep it that way. Anybody could see that. But most of my experiences with white people had been good ones. Mama worked for some nice white folks, the Gunsons, who gave us presents at Christmas and hand-me-down clothes all year. They even gave Mama a car—Mrs. Gunson's real nice car that they could have traded. They were good people who cared about Mama and the rest of our family. My direct experiences had told me that white people were all right—until one Monday afternoon when I was thirteen.

Right after school that Monday I read the headlines on the *Atlanta Journal*, just like I did every afternoon before I rode through my west Atlanta neighborhood delivering papers. Lately everything had been about the French in Indochina, someplace I hadn't learned about yet in geography. The issue was whether the United States would help them with a war over there. I never took time to read the articles, just the headlines and sometimes "Street Scenes," a short front-page column of unusual items submitted by readers. But on that Tuesday, I read every word, and I truly believed something exciting was about to happen—that new opportunities would open for me and my neighborhood friends.

"Court Kills Segregation in Schools," the headline read. The first line of the article explained, "The Supreme Court today unanimously outlawed racial segregation in public schools." I was going to school with white children, a possibility I never could have dreamed on my own. As I read the article, I wondered what their schools must be like. They probably got new books every year instead of the torn and tattered ones like we used, and maybe even new desks.

The bad news lay in the second line of the headline, which read, "Cheap Politics, Talmadge Retorts." I looked closely at the picture of Governor Herman Talmadge standing in front of several microphones. As calm as a principal reading the lunch menu, he said he wanted "permanent segregation of the races" in Georgia. We were just learning in school how the judicial, legislative, and executive branches are divided, and how the states and the federal government have certain powers. But it seemed to me that if the United States Supreme Court said it, the governor couldn't stop it. I wondered why he would want to stop it in the first place, and who else would stand with him.

After I delivered the papers that afternoon, Melvin Rivers and I rode our bicycles up the hill on Simpson Road toward Tiger Flowers's big house, a twenty-room stucco and brick mansion that sat empty. Tiger had been the first black man to win the world middleweight boxing championship back in 1926, and the next year he moved into his new house—like nothing else in the neighborhood.

Less than a year later Tiger died. I don't know how long the house had been empty, but I wanted to see inside. When Melvin and I reached the circular drive in front, I looked up and down the street to see if anybody would see us if we rode up to the front door.

That's when a big 1940 Ford, black with a long, wide dusty hood, pulled along beside me and slowed. A white man was driving. Few of the white men I saw in the neighborhood ever spoke to me, so I wasn't sure what he wanted or why he was slowing. For an instant he reminded me of the picture of Governor Talmadge, with his hair combed back and his slightly puffy cheeks, except he wasn't wearing a suit. Then it was like he pulled off a mask. I saw that he hadn't shaved that day, and his lips were brown and crusty with tobacco juice as he worked his jaw slowly up and down. He didn't ask for directions. He didn't say anything. Instead, he tightened his cheeks, pursed his dirty lips, and leaned out the car window to get just a little closer to me. Then his eyes grew big and white like a dog's ready to fight. I wanted to run—to jump on my bike and ride away—but my legs wouldn't move. I was afraid to run, afraid he might chase me or hit me with his big car, so I watched his white eyes until the brown spit hit my cheek, and then the man threw his head against the back of the seat and laughed wildly as he hit the gas hard and spun rocks at my feet. I was frozen, gazing at the empty space where the car had been.

When you're thirteen years old and a man—a total stranger—spits in your face, all you can do is cry. At least, that's all I could do. I might have vowed to get even someday with every white man in Atlanta. I could have written down the man's license number and told my father so he could track him down. But I didn't do those things.

I had to collect myself just to be able to lay down my bicycle and sit in the grass beside the sidewalk. I looked at Melvin and he didn't say anything. Who knew what to say? I had been introduced to this ugly side of the world. I wasn't going to school with any children of that white man. I didn't want to. Anyway, he would see me dead before that happened.

Melvin rode off. He couldn't do anything for me at that point. I touched the spit with my hand to wipe it off, and I winced. I wiped my hand on my pants, and then I pulled the front of my shirt up and wiped my face. The ugly brown stain fell right over the middle of my stomach. Without standing, I turned and crawled behind a big bush and cried.

I'm not sure I'd ever heard the words "stay in your place," but that's what the spit must have meant. Even if I'd heard it, I'm not sure it would have bothered me much, for up to that time, "my place" wasn't so bad. I had plenty of family around, including five brothers and sisters along with my parents and grandparents, and with money from throwing papers and other odd jobs, I felt financially independent.

Most of our neighbors in the area west of Vine City between Hunter and Simpson streets were blue-collar workers, although many were college educated. A few of those with degrees were professionals or schoolteachers; others worked at the post office. As a child I was unaware that college-educated men were being locked out of employment because their skin was black. I did not realize we black folks had a "place." And, as time went by, the more I saw of white people and their place for me, the less I liked either of them.

After I wiped the spit from my face and rode my bicycle home, I was relieved to find the house empty. My mother and father were at work, and my brother and sisters were out playing. I could wash my face and shirt without any questions.

The cool water at the bathroom sink ran down my arms and splashed on my bare chest as I rubbed my face hard again and again. I blew out my mouth with each splash to avoid the possibility of any lingering taste. Then I dried my face and hands with a clean towel. Not until I went to my room for another shirt did I see my reflection in a mirror. I walked slowly toward the dresser and examined my face—the corners of my eyes, my hairline—then my head. All clean. All gone. But still I could feel the spit. I sat on the bed, then lay back and closed my eyes. Instead of the relief I had expected, my mind took me once again to an earlier, awful day—the day I thought my father was dead.

I must have been just four or five years old when it happened. They brought my father home so badly beaten I couldn't see how he could be alive. He couldn't walk. Couldn't see. Couldn't talk. His bloody face and swollen eyes didn't move when they put him on his bed. Then they made me leave the room, and I didn't see him again until late the next day. By then, he could barely open his eyes. He still didn't speak. He just lay there on the bed.

When he was able to talk again, he said he had beaten with clubs for no reason. Some white men had made up a story about him sassing a white woman in a crosswalk, and she supposedly went home and told her husband, who was an Atlanta policeman. Then they hunted my father down like an animal and beat him.

My family didn't discuss the incident in front of me during the intervening years, and I had tried to push it to the outer edge of my memory, until I wondered if it hadn't been a dream or something I'd made up. Why, after all, would somebody beat up my father with no provocation?

Now I knew it was true. And I wondered when it would happen to me.

I didn't feel like leaving the house at that point, but I had told Henry Stone that I would meet him at Washington Park to play tennis that afternoon. Henry, known by most as "Junior," was one of my closest friends. I picked up my racquet, went outside, climbed on my bicycle, and rode over to the park.

Washington Park was the only "colored" park in Atlanta—one of the oldest ones in the country, in fact. It was there, on that afternoon, that I began to see through new eyes how the system worked—how the system provided black people just enough recreation, just enough education, just enough money to keep them from marching down Peachtree Street and demanding their due. The evidence had been there all my life. I just hadn't thought seriously about it until now. I had heard black people say they weren't satisfied with their limited choices. They wanted to walk through Piedmont Park without going to jail, to eat lunch and try on clothes at Rich's, and attend any school in town. On May 17, 1954, for the first time, I wanted those things, too.

Junior and I took one of the three dirt courts that backed up to the back fence. He pulled out of his pocket three obviously discarded, bald, soft tennis balls that he had picked up somewhere. We were just three or four games into the set when the adults started showing up. Washington Park was a great gathering place for the neighborhood. I think Mama was glad I took up tennis, because she knew it would help me stay out of trouble. Schoolteachers and administrators, policemen, and janitors all talked and laughed while they waited their turn to play. And they didn't mind intimidating younger players. At five o'clock, they believed, the courts belonged to them.

"Okay, boys, time's up," said J. D. Hudson, an ex-police officer who later became the city's corrections commissioner.

Junior put the tennis balls in his pocket and headed for the sideline, but I wasn't ready to stop. We hadn't finished our set.

"Not yet," I said. "Let us finish this set. Come on back, Junior."

"Get on out of here, Bo," Hudson said a little louder. "Your time's up."

I took his raised voice as a challenge and turned to face him. "My Dad's tax dollars paid for this court," I said, "and I'm going to stay till we finish this set." Junior was off the court already.

Hudson raised his racquet and stepped quickly toward me. "You'll get your butt out of here right now," he said.

I called him a name and he chased me. He probably would have beaten me if he could have caught me, but I was fast when I was thirteen. It made me angry though, that so many of us were forced to share that one little park. It just wasn't fair.

Even so, tennis became an increasingly important part of my life as a teenager. For two summers, I attended a tennis camp operated by Warren Memorial Methodist Church where Ralph Long, Sr., coached us. My high school mathematics teacher, Marshall Arnold, also worked with us as our tennis coach.

Branch Curington was one of the better players at the park. I watched in awe when he served, his left arm rising slowly to release the ball, which seemed to stop and wait for him to extend fully and slam the racquet against it. He should have been able to go anywhere he wanted, and yet, less than a year later he would give up tennis completely. Just walk away from it. And when I heard him explain why, I wondered why he had worked so hard at it in the first place.

As a teenager, Branch had worked at the Piedmont Driving Club, an elite, segregated Atlanta social club, watering, dragging, and marking the tennis courts every day. Younger blacks worked at the Driving Club as ball boys. That's how we got most of our tennis balls at Washington Park—Driving Club castoffs.

Branch picked up the game and over time learned quite a bit from the teaching pro—so much so, in fact, that after a few years he was giving lessons to Driving Club members.

One time the *Atlanta Journal* carried an item in its "Street Scenes" column: "Seen from the bus in Ansley Park: Negro playing tennis on the courts at the Piedmont Driving Club," and everybody in the neighborhood knew it had to be Branch.

Branch's busiest time would be in winter, when the regular pro spent several months in Florida. Branch said he enjoyed instructing or playing tennis with members.

But he explained later, "No matter what my role was, no matter what I did, I was just a servant to people with money. That's the way it was with all the employees at the Driving Club. If one of the members asked you to do some yard work for them at their home, you did it and took whatever money they offered—not because you needed the work or the money, but because you couldn't afford to let them think you were 'uppity.' And when the members' sons turned twelve, I had to call them 'sir,' no matter what, or risk losing tips, or worse."

I lived with the same humiliation in the 1950s when I worked as a waiter at the Driving Club, and I swore I would never work there as an adult. I saw black men who had marched to the tune for years, and I wondered how they lived with themselves.

When Branch married and started a family, he decided the Driving Club was no place for him. "I was going home every day feeling like less than a man," he said.

He thought things were changing when the tennis pro left the Cherokee Country Club, another elite, segregated club, and the president asked him to interview for the position. "They offered me a job with a guaranteed salary," he said. "I was going to be the man. It was a one-in-a-million shot—a black tennis pro at the Cherokee Country Club in the 1950s. They knew I was a good teacher, and they came looking for me. But then they said they were hiring me as assistant pro. I asked them, 'Well, if I'm going to be the only one teaching, why don't you make me the pro? Whose assistant will I be?'"

When they couldn't answer, Branch decided that was another bad deal. He reflected on what a white friend had told him several years earlier: "Learn all you can about tennis, then leave the South. You'll never have an opportunity there."

But Branch's mother lived in Atlanta, and all his ties were here. So he stayed, and he gave up tennis and got a job running a filling station and grocery store. And when he saw a boy like me, thirteen years old with some potential, he said, "Yeah, he'll go to college. Maybe get a job teaching or working at the post office, or both if he wants to do better."

Because that's what black folk did. That's all the opportunity we had in Georgia in 1954. We couldn't even stand up for our rights without risking further limitations on our freedom.

In those days, I worked during the Christmas holidays delivering packages for Davison's on Peachtree Street. People who worked downtown would come into the store during the day and buy Christmas presents, and then after the presents were wrapped I would carry them to the customers' offices.

During a break one day, I walked up the street to Reeder & McGaughey Sporting Goods to look at jackets. They had a dozen or more different colors, but I liked one that was black and yellow. I didn't have enough money to pay for it yet, so I put a few dollars down and they held it on layaway.

A few weeks later, I had saved enough money to get my jacket. I met a co-worker from Davison's who walked with me to the sporting goods store, where I paid the man for my jacket and slipped it on. It felt good, and it looked good. I couldn't wait to wear it to school the next day. I hadn't seen another one quite like it.

We walked back to work at Davison's, and a white boy who also delivered packages pointed at me and said, "Hey, you!"

I stopped. He was clearly upset about something, but I couldn't imagine what.

"You take that jacket off!" he demanded.

His sudden, unexplained fury stunned me.

"What are you talking about?" I asked.

"You heard me. Take off that jacket. Those are Sylvan High colors. You can't wear that."

"I just bought this jacket and I'm not about to take it off."

"I don't care who paid for it," he said, "you're wearing Sylvan High colors, and I don't like it."

He kept on about it until my friend said to the boy, "You're going to mess around and get your ass kicked."

23

It was an option I hadn't considered. We were downtown in the late 1950s, where a couple of African-American students might have found themselves in jail for whipping a white boy. This was just another reminder of what we were up against.

Two more frightening and potentially discouraging incidents of my growing-up years involved Atlanta policemen. I delivered the *Atlanta Journal* every day—all the way into my college career. On Sundays, I'd get up long before the sun rose, usually at about 4:30, and walk to the corner where K. C. Marks left a stack of papers for me to deliver. I used wire cutters to loosen the bundle so I could pull out the papers and sling them up to the doors of my customers.

It must have been twenty-five degrees one winter morning and I was bundled in a coat and gloves and hat and walking toward my stack of papers when, about a block from home, I saw headlights coming toward me. I glanced up and saw that it was a police car, so I put my head down and kept pedaling. Next thing I knew the car had stopped at the curb across the street and I heard, "Hey, boy!"

I was about fifteen years old at the time, and already bigger than many men, but I wasn't surprised to be called "boy" by a white Atlanta policeman. In fact, my father wouldn't have been surprised if a white man called him "boy." Angry. Insulted. Degraded. But not surprised.

So I stopped on my side of the street and turned toward the policeman. "Yes, sir?"

Then he said, as if I should have followed his order before he even made it, "Git yore black ass over here!"

I walked over to his car and he looked me over, up and down, front and back.

"Whatcha got in your back pocket there?"

"Wire cutters. I throw papers. Have to cut the wire bundles."

"Take 'em out real slow."

I put one hand in the air and reached back with the other to pull the wire cutters from my pocket.

"Drop 'em on the ground and put your hands on the car."

I followed his instructions, and he proceeded to pat me down. Finding nothing incriminating, he said, "Now get your black ass out of here," as if it were his neighborhood and I was not allowed.

Several months later, at the same time of day, I was walking against traffic near the curb on Proctor Street—there was no sidewalk—carrying my newspapers on my back. A police car came toward me from several blocks away, and as the car neared me the policeman swerved and drove right toward me. I jumped up onto the curb, and the car came close enough for me that I could see two men in uniform laughing and bobbing up and down like little kids at the carnival. I was a game to those men—just a game like a cat with a mouse, and they didn't care what their enjoyment cost me.

You would think that the denial of so many basic rights to African-Americans would have encouraged us to form a cohesive community to work together. Unfortunately, however, our community, like all others, experienced its own divisions and exclusions. As the son of blue-collar working class people, I was often left out of social occasions sponsored by the community's doctors, professors, and attorneys. There was a not-so-subtle division among the classes, and those parents did not want their sons and daughters socializing with members of families who, in their minds, had not climbed high enough up the social ladder.

There were a lot of hurt feelings within the African-American community during my growing-up years. Young people were excluded from parties or groups simply because their parents were not college educated or they did not appear to be of the correct social stratum. Lawrence Otis Graham, a nationally known attorney and commentator on race, politics, and class in America, explored this phenomenon in depth in his book *Our Kind of People*. Graham writes that status-related cliques formed for honorable reasons, primarily because wealthy blacks were denied access to clubs in the white population. One result of this exclusivity within our own community, however, was further denial of opportunity to many, in some cases for the simple reason that our skin was too dark. I still cannot understand how groups within the African-American community can fight segregation on the one hand and embrace it on the other.

During those difficult times, my friend Hamilton Holmes earned my deepest respect. Hamp's grandfather, Dr. Hamilton Mayo Holmes, had been a prominent black Atlanta physician. His son, Alfred "Tup" Holmes, was a successful businessman who won a US Supreme Court case desegregating Atlanta's public golf courses in 1956 (I later proposed the naming of Alfred "Tup" Holmes Golf Course in Atlanta), and his mother came from a prominent family involved in Tuskegee Institute in Alabama.

Because of his background, and his polite demeanor, Hamp was included in almost every social function for teenagers. But he didn't always accept. When a party or other social function included him and excluded some of his friends, Hamp often declined the invitation.

"If Marvin can't come," I heard him say more than once, "then I won't be coming either."

Hamp's family honored me by inviting me to speak at his funeral in 1995. As I said then, he was a prince of a gentleman, and the smartest man I ever knew.

Even though I didn't find out about it until more than twenty years after the incident, there was a time in high school when even Hamp disappointed me. I don't know why he did it; I never asked him. I was the quarterback on the football team at Henry M. Turner High School. Hamp was the co-captain of the team. We had won our first four or five football games that season and were preparing to play Howard High School from Chattanooga. We kicked off, and as I got ready to go in, Coach Williams said, "Arrington, you're not starting tonight."

I could not understand that, but in those days, you'd get your head knocked off your shoulders if you questioned a coach. Finally, after the second-string quarterback had failed horribly, the coach told me to go in there and get us back in the ballgame. I was able to get things turned around, and we won the game.

Twenty-five years later, a mutual friend of ours (mine and Hamp's), George B. Smith, III, dropped by my house during the Christmas season and said, "Man, something has been on my heart over the years and I just wanted to make my peace with you."

I said, "What's wrong, Smitty?"

George said, "The reason you didn't start the Howard High football game is that a group of us, including Hamp, went to Coach and said we had lost confidence in you. It was the wrong thing to do and we never should have done it."

Still, he could not explain why they did it. Smitty told me this before Hamp died, and I debated whether to mention it to him because so much time had elapsed and I considered him a very close and dear friend. I decided it was more important to preserve our friendship than bring up an issue that was in the past. We were all young, and young people do foolish things. You learn to forgive and forget.

I had long felt that even within my own community people were trying to relegate me to "my place"—a lower rung on the social ladder. So, I began to act the part. I was streetwise and quick to fight. Many of my buddies distinguished themselves with criminal records, and I enjoyed the status that came with being tough and having a foul mouth. I think in one sense I hung out with those guys and held onto my tough reputation because I felt like I belonged among the poor.

I became known as someone who wouldn't be pushed around, and I didn't like to see my friends pushed around either. I once coaxed my good friend Lowell Dickerson into a fight with a bully, Homer Pope, who had taken a basketball away from him. "Brother,"

I told Lowell, "if you don't stand up for yourself, nobody else will." Lowell won the fight and learned to stand up for himself.

As we moved toward high school graduation, however, we turned toward more serious matters. Our homecoming queen, Charlayne Hunter, along with my good friend, Hamilton Holmes, class valedictorian, would soon take on the entire state and even the region by challenging laws that excluded African-Americans from the University of Georgia. Others of us fought for integration by marching through the streets of Atlanta and sitting in at lunch counters all over town.

More than any other experience of my college years, the student protests of the early 1960s are burned into my memory. For the first time in our young lives, we were taking control of our destinies. We weren't going to let anybody else tell us what we could and could not do with our lives.

Student leaders like Ben Brown, Julian Bond, James Felder, Carolyn Long Banks, Annie Ruth Borders, Danny Mitchell, Charles Black, Marion Wright Edelman, Herschelle Sullivan, and Morris Dillard inspired us by the hundreds to take to the streets in nonviolent marches and risk arrest by sitting in at local restaurants that refused service to African Americans.

They and other leaders met regularly at Paschal's restaurant, the unofficial headquarters of the movement in Atlanta. When others were afraid to host the meetings of freedom riders, picketers, and boycotters, Paschal Brothers welcomed them.

When I think of the student movement in Atlanta, Lonnie King's name comes to mind before all others. Lonnie was a few years older than I. He and my brother Joe were close—so close, in fact, that Joe is godfather to Lonnie's son.

I particularly remember Lonnie as the primary organizer of the movement beginning in February 1960, in the middle of my freshman year at Clark College. He picked up a newspaper on

February 2 and read that four black college freshmen had sat down at a whites-only lunch counter in Greensboro, North Carolina. That incident triggered a desire that had burned inside Lonnie for years. I can still see him standing up in the Atlanta University Center and telling us, "Those folks in Greensboro shouldn't be doing this alone. Segregation is ubiquitous, and we don't have to live with it anymore."

The next thing we knew, Lonnie and Julian Bond were organizing for similar demonstrations in Atlanta.

Lonnie's preparation for leadership began in 1954 when he graduated from high school and joined the Navy. Three months after the *Brown v. Board of Education* decision, Lonnie experienced for the first time the openness of society outside the South. At boot camp in Great Lakes, Michigan, he scored so high on his General Classification Test (GCT) that the Navy made him an educational petty officer for a group of eighty men. One of his primary responsibilities was to tutor men, all of them white and most from the South, who had failed the GCT. For eleven weeks he worked, and when his men took the test again, all eighty of them passed.

While they prepared to be retested, the men held weekly table tennis tournaments, with the winner receiving a carton of cigarettes. Lonnie, who didn't smoke, won all eleven tournaments. So every week the guys came to him for smokes. You can imagine, then, that after nearly three months Lonnie had earned the respect of virtually all of his men.

That respect would be tested when, given leave, they came South from boot camp. Lonnie rode the train with eight or ten of the men from Michigan to Ohio. Then, as they pulled out of Cincinnati, the conductor came over and told Lonnie he would have to move to the Negro car.

"No sir," said one of Lonnie's white companions. "If Lonnie has to go, we're going with him."

The conductor tried to prevail upon the men to follow the rules, but they refused. Rather than risk the spectacle of a bunch of white

Navy enlistees integrating the Negro car, the conductor said, "Ah, to heck with it," and let Lonnie stay in the white car to Atlanta.

When Lonnie reported to his ship in San Diego a week later, he once again stared discrimination in the face. After a two-week orientation as part of a group of forty men, the personnel officer made assignments. Some men became electrical technicians or fire controllers. Lonnie, who had the highest GCT score among the forty men, and a guy from Kentucky who had the lowest, were assigned to chip paint.

"It was clear to me the only difference was that I was black," Lonnie would say later. "Thirty-eight white guys with lower GCT scores got career-enhancing assignments, and I was chipping paint. You think they would send a white guy with the highest score to chip paint? I knew something was wrong with that."

But Lonnie also knew there was nothing much he could do about individual racist attitudes in the military, so he went out with the guy from Kentucky and chipped paint.

It wasn't long before Lonnie received a new assignment—cleaning bathrooms. This time he worked alone. And he was mad.

"Then I remembered something Benjamin Mays [longtime president of Morehouse College] said," Lonnie recalled later. "He said, 'Even if you have to be a garbage man, be the best garbage man there is.' So I decided to clean those bathrooms like nobody would believe. And after a few days I had them so clean, I just had to go in early to do a little bit, then I could take off the rest of the morning. I was effectively working an hour a day and reading the rest of the time."

Then a third-class petty officer, seeing how apparently easy Lonnie's job had become, applied for it and took it from him.

By the time Lonnie earned his discharge, he was ready to change the world. When a friend of his asked why he was going back South, back to even greater discrimination, Lonnie said, "Things are going to change in the South and I want to be there and be a part of it."

It would be three more years before I would see Lonnie King attending Morehouse College on a football scholarship. Standing up in the Atlanta University Center, he called us to action, and we were ready. The time was right, and we were ready to move.

Lonnie came to me that afternoon and asked me to help with marches and demonstrations. I told him I was ready.

Then he told me what would be required. "We have to be nonviolent," he said, "no matter what. If somebody hits you, you have to take it. You can't strike back."

I had been a fighter all my life to that point, a defender of myself and my rights. I said, "I'm not sure I can be nonviolent in that instance. I won't provoke anything, but if somebody hits me, I'm going to hit back."

Lonnie explained that if we had a confrontation that led to black males fist-fighting white males, we soon would see people lining up with guns. "You have to be a victim to conquer," he said. "You have to be a victim."

That's where Lonnie and some of my classmates were stronger than I, and I had to limit my role in the sit-in demonstrations. That non-violent philosophy was tough for me in those days. I was off of Ashby and Simpson Streets where everybody had a big knife in his pocket. I had my knife like everybody else. The idea that if people did nasty, horrible things to us we were just supposed to take it wasn't a part of my makeup. Also, our football coach at Clark, Leonidas Epps, one of the greatest people I've ever known, told us that what the students were doing was noble, but that he didn't want his football players involved, because he didn't want any of us to get locked up. So, I kind of used that as an excuse, too.

And, after I saw my daddy get beaten like that when I was a child, I didn't want to go through anymore of that. Lonnie kept telling us that if we didn't have the discipline to show restraint, then don't do it. I've often regretted not being able to fully participate in the sit-ins, but I did take part in the marches. The cause was that important.

It wasn't long before hundreds of students from Clark, Morehouse, Morris Brown, Spelman, Atlanta University, and the Interdenominational Theological Center were ready to march. Before we could hit the streets, Dr. Mays sent his secretary to find Lonnie and invited him to his office. When he arrived, all of the college presidents were sitting at a conference table. Other students, also invited by Dr. Mays, stood around the room. Dr. Rufus Clement, president of Atlanta University, began the discussion by explaining that he and the other college presidents certainly believed in, and sympathized with, our goals, but . . ..

It seems there's always a "but," followed by a reason good people shouldn't do the right thing.

"But we think you ought to go back to class and let the NAACP handle matters," Dr. Clement said. "They're much better equipped for it."

The students in the room deferred to Lonnie, who had led them so far.

"With all due respect, gentlemen," Lonnie said, "the time has come for us to end segregation in public accommodations. We go downtown to spend our money, and we can't even try on clothes. We can't eat in the restaurants; they put us somewhere down by the restrooms. In some places a woman who is pregnant and tired can't even sit down."

"Are you prepared to sacrifice your education if it doesn't go as planned?" one of the school presidents asked Lonnie.

"Some of us are prepared to sacrifice our education in this struggle," Lonnie said. "There will have to be victims, and some of us are prepared to do that."

"Are you prepared to die?" Dr. Mays asked.

The other students all looked to Lonnie and waited. "I can't speak for anyone else," Lonnie said, "but I am."

Several heads nodded in agreement.

When the presidents realized how serious the students were, they offered their support and advice.

"Then I'd like to see you write a statement asking for redress of your grievances," Dr. Mays said. "If you're planning to attack a man, you should state clearly why in a manifesto. Tell him, 'I am attacking you for the following reasons,' then attack."

Dr. Clement suggested the students run a full-page ad in the newspaper. He even offered to raise money to pay for it to run in all three of the local daily papers, the *Atlanta Constitution*, the *Atlanta Journal*, and the *Atlanta Inquirer*. The effect was chilling. On March 9, 1960, Atlantans awoke to "An Appeal for Human Rights." In a well-written declaration of intent, Lonnie and Julian Bond had laid out the issues regarding segregation in education, jobs, housing, voting, hospitals, public facilities, and law enforcement. The ad read in part,

We hold that:

1. The practice of racial segregation is not in keeping with ideals of Democracy and Christianity.

2. Racial segregation is robbing not only the segregated but the segregator of his human dignity. Furthermore, the propagation of racial prejudice is unfair to the generations yet unborn.

3. In times of war, the Negro has fought and died for his country; yet he still has not been accorded first-class citizenship.

4. In spite of the fact that the Negro pays his share of taxes, he does not enjoy participation in city, county and state government at the level where laws are enacted.

5. The social, economic, and political progress of Georgia is retarded by segregation and prejudices.

6. America is fast losing the respect of other nations by the poor example which she sets in the area of race relations.

Responding to a lack of action in alleviating segregation, the students pledged to "use every legal and non-violent means at our disposal to secure full citizenship rights as members of this great Democracy of ours."

Response was swift and predictable. Governor Ernest Vandiver, in published remarks, ensured that even more students would participate.

"The statement was skillfully prepared," he wrote. "Obviously, it was not written by students.... It did not sound like it was prepared in any Georgia school or college; nor, in fact, did it read like it was written even in this country. This left-wing statement is calculated to breed dissatisfaction, discontent, discord, and evil."

What the governor obviously did not understand was that it was his own stance against integration that bred "discontent, discord, and evil." While he and many others believed all was well among black people, the students' appeal stated otherwise: "The time has come for the people of Atlanta and Georgia to take a good look at what is really happening in this country, and to stop believing those who tell us that everything is fine and equal, and that the Negro is happy and satisfied."

Two months later, virtually the entire student bodies of all six of our colleges decided to make a peaceful statement to the governor regarding our position. Lonnie called for all of us to meet at the Atlanta University quadrangle on May 17, 1960, then to march to the state Capitol. Four thousand students showed up, and again Dr. Mays sent his secretary to summon Lonnie. This time Dr. Mays had his wife, whom we called "Miss Sadie," at his side. Lonnie reported that they both looked extremely worried.

Dr. Mays told Lonnie he thought the students were marching toward big trouble this time. Governor Vandiver had called out the state troopers with their billy clubs to surround the Capitol.

Lonnie said Dr. Mays told him, "I just talked to the city's police chief, Herbert Jenkins, and he said they can't protect the students."

Then Miss Sadie told him, "Lonnie, I want you to turn those students around and go back to class."

Lonnie refused. "Dr. Mays," he said, "let me take you to a speech you made in chapel when I was a sophomore—a speech entitled 'Never Sacrifice a Principle for Peace.' Do you remember that?"

Dr. Mays said he did.

"You also said we should prepare ourselves for leadership one day. Well, today the principle is integration, and for me to call off this march when we are protesting segregation would be to sacrifice a principle for peace. With all due respect for you, I cannot do that."

Dr. Mays then offered a compromise, asking the students to bypass the Capitol by a block and march to Wheat Street Baptist Church on Auburn Avenue. Lonnie agreed to consider a route change. We marched up Hunter Street toward the Capitol. When we got nearly to Forsyth Street, Police Chief Herbert Jenkins stopped us and called us over. He said, "It's going to be a massacre in this town today, and I don't want it to happen on my watch."

We could see state troopers up ahead with their billy sticks, just waiting for us. We started out again, but when we got to Mitchell and Forsyth, Lonnie directed us to turn left, and we went past Rich's and proceeded over to Auburn Avenue.

Downtown, there were so many spectators out there—white folks screaming, hollering, using the N-word, telling us to go home. Chief Jenkins had the police to kind of protect us on this new route and, thank God, there was no bloodbath that day. I was so scared my knees shook the whole way, but we made our point peacefully.

Looking back, it's easier to understand how the college presidents must have felt. They had lived with segregation all their lives, and probably wanted integration even more than we did. At the same time, they were our custodians, responsible for our very lives. How could they explain to parents in Chicago or Philadelphia if a child had been killed during a protest?

What Lonnie was asking us to do was hypnotic. Change had to come, and we knew we could make it come fast. And we did. As the movement won little victories—an open lunch counter here, a discarded "colored" sign there—more people joined. The time was incredibly challenging—a defining moment in the lives of many of us.

Still, the reality of being black in a city controlled by whites could never be forgotten. As a student at Clark College, I often studied at the home of my friend Edward Scoggin on Proctor Street. Edward was four years older than I was, and his apartment was usually quieter and more conducive to studying than our house.

Walking home from Edward's one night about nine o'clock, a police car was driving slowly up Cairo Street. Its blue lights came on, and I knew it was coming for me. I considered running, but the officer could have shot me in the back, so I kept walking with my books under my arm. The car pulled over to the curb, and the white policeman stepped out and raised his revolver.

Shaking in my shoes, I froze with my hands at my sides, wondering if he would shoot me dead on the sidewalk.

"Where you coming from, boy?" he demanded.

"Studying at a friend's house," I said raising my books for him to see. "I'm walking home. I'm a college student."

He studied me carefully then, without lowering the pistol, said, "You go on."

I walked the rest of the way home knowing things had to change. That fall, I saw another example of the kind of courage it would take to implement that change. The Clark College football team was traveling to New Orleans for a football game, and the bus stopped at in Mississippi for food and a bathroom break. When Jim Felder, our quarterback and captain, saw that the facility was segregated—that we would have to get our food out of the back door and use "colored" bathroom facilities, he refused to get off the bus.

The way it worked was, you go around back, knock on the door, and the lady would serve you, whatever you wanted. A bunch of us on the offensive unit were rushing to get some food. We were hungry. I used to call Fielder "homeboy." I said, "Homeboy, you're not going to get any food?"

He said, "No, man. That's not dignified. I pay my money so somebody can serve me out the back door? I just won't eat. I will not support segregation."

The rest of us got strength when he said that. As hungry as we were, we decided not to get food, either. Homeboy was our quarterback, one of the co-captains and the president of the student body at Clark. We looked up to him. We knew he was right.

To prevail in our struggle, we had to be willing to endure many trials.

A few years later, as the city of Atlanta continued to undergo tremendous change, I would get my chance to be a part of that change. Lonnie King graduated from Morehouse, and we lost contact for several years. But in 1968, the NAACP asked him to head up the Atlanta chapter. He got involved in city politics and convinced me to run for a seat on the Atlanta Board of Aldermen.

At about that same time, after I graduated from Emory University Law School, another great opportunity arose. Student unrest was escalating around the country, and Emory was not immune. The growing number of black students there had staged a protest, and the administration was eager to improve its relationship with them. Emory was planning to establish the position of student personnel adviser and fill it with the school's first black administrator.

While I was eating lunch at the Morrison's in Midtown one afternoon (allowed because we had marched a few years earlier), I ran into Elridge McMillan, a fellow Clark alumnus. Elridge had recently left a position as chief of the education branch of the federal Office for Civil Rights, and now was the associate director of the Southern Education Foundation. Elridge told me to call Thomas Fernandez at Emory about the new position. I immediately contacted Fernandez, and my interview with him led to a job offer. So, as I continued to learn city politics through the election process, I also began to find my way around university administration.

I functioned, in essence, as the dean of Emory's two hundred or so black students, coordinating their activities, recruiting more black students, and helping to establish one of the first black studies programs. Later I was proud to help recruit Dr. Delores Aldridge to head the black studies program. Delores had been valedictorian of my graduating class at Clark College in 1963.

I continued my work as student personnel adviser at Emory University, attracting bright young African Americans to campus. We recruited the top high school students, the ones we believed could succeed in Emory's rigorous academic program. Of course, as a private institution, Emory might have been much more expensive than many African-American students and their families could afford, but the university has always had money, and it was generous with scholarships or loans to worthy students. No outstanding African American was turned away for a lack of money.

At the same time, we tried to maintain a sense of serenity in the midst of war protests as similar demonstrations on other campuses across the country ended in violence. One of the more tense moments came when a group of student protesters lowered an American flag from the flagpole and threatened to burn it.

They were on the quadrangle, that sylvan lawn surrounded by stately marble buildings. They made a lot of noise and quickly attracted a crowd that included students who had served in Vietnam, as well as faculty members who emerged from their offices. The veterans said that if the protesters burned that flag, it would be a day that Atlantans would remember for the rest of their lives—a thinly veiled threat of violence.

One student whose short hair implied recent military service made the point more emphatically: "They are not going to burn the American flag."

I knew he wasn't bluffing, and the last thing we wanted on campus was a bunch of veterans beating up student protesters. So I walked up to one of the students with the flag and said firmly, "Man, let me have that flag before you start a riot."

Mine was one of the few black faces in the crowd, but that didn't matter to me or to either group of students. The student clutched the flag more tightly and stared in defiance.

I stared hard into the student's eyes so there would be no misunderstanding, and said, "You don't know what you're about to get started here, and once it starts none of us will be able to stop it. Now you let me have that flag."

With that, he folded the flag up and he gave it to me. I put it under my arm, then turned and walked to my office through the dispersing crowd. I closed my door and almost passed out from relief. If they had burned that flag that day, all Hell would have broken loose.

That incident would not be the only controversial event on the Emory campus during my tenure. An invitation for a group of Black Panthers to speak on campus might have been equally explosive anywhere else in DeKalb County, but at Emory we avoided any unrest. When several administrators told me they thought the invitation was inappropriate and would incite students, I explained that in my law school classes we had discussed freedom of speech at length, and we had to allow the Panthers, or any other group, a forum. If students invited Ku Klux Klan members for a similar address, I would have to support it.

"I can disagree with a certain philosophy and still allow a person or group to speak," I said.

The administrators could have overruled me, but they did not. The Panthers came to campus and stayed for three or four hours, then moved on. Because we hadn't made a big deal about it, the event went almost unnoticed.

Even as we demanded an integrated society, a group of African-American students asked me to help them rent a house on Clifton Road, north of campus, where they could party on weekend nights.

I asked why no white students were a part of their group.

"We just want to be with our brothers and sisters," they said.

"This is nothing but segregation," I said. "I thought we were trying to integrate."

"This is different," they said. "We just want to party."

I'm not sure they ever saw my point, but I helped them get the place, which they called the Black House.

On the Emory campus, though, life really was different. On many days I was relieved to drive through the Emory gate, where I always felt protected. I didn't have to worry about anybody following me or asking why I was driving through their all-white neighborhood.

Additionally, we had true giants associated with the university, people like Henry L. Bowden, Sr., chairman of the Emory Board of Trustees and Atlanta city attorney since the days of Mayor Hartsfield. Mr. Bowden took an interest in me as a student, an administrator, and as an alderman from the very first day I won my election. He made it clear he wanted me and every other Emory graduate to succeed, and he gave me all the love and care that he would give to his own son.

Likewise, Judson C. "Jake" Ward took a particular interest in my success. He was one of those kind, wise educators who never told me I was wrong, but would suggest sometimes that I look at issues from a different perspective.

Sometimes, though, the issue was so obvious there was only one way to see it. The student protest movement and its larger counterpart, the civil rights movement, changed the legal nature of racism, but its cultural component remained intact, and even strengthened with the conservative counterrevolution of the 1980s. "My place," once defined by laws and customs, became defined by unrepentant individual behavior and a political atmosphere and leadership that paved the way for this reality.

Nearly a decade after the student movement had swept the country, African Americans were only beginning to make inroads against a society that had been segregated for centuries.

During my first term on the board of aldermen, Henry Dodson (who once served on the Fulton County Commission) came to me with disturbing news. A black businessman had called him and reported that the Atlanta Water Works was still thoroughly segregated. Dodson and I went to check this out and paid a visit to the Howell Mill Road facility.

Paul Weir, who otherwise had run the water works well, confirmed the report. He said the white and black employees had separate restroom facilities and dressing rooms. Not only that, they had separate water buckets on city trucks.

Enraged, I said the segregation had to end.

"But they like it like this," Weir protested.

"The walls come down," I said, "or I'll be back with a sledge hammer and physically bring them down myself."

Weir said he would consider the matter, but was clearly in no hurry to make changes. Maynard Jackson, who had been elected the city's first black vice-mayor, then joined Dodson and me in demanding immediate integration. After heated debate, the Public Works Committee ordered a complete overhaul of the old system, including the assignment of lockers on a strictly alphabetical basis.

No longer were there "white" and "colored" water buckets on the trucks. Everyone drank from the same tap.

In the fall of 1972, the African American community took another cold slap from the State Board of Bar Examiners, which controlled who practiced law in Georgia. Every black applicant who took the bar examination in November that year failed. Many of those people had attended some of the best law schools: Yale, Emory, and the University of Georgia. The situation was inexcusable, and I decided to address it through the legal system. The American Civil Liberties Union had the same idea, so we sued the all-white State Board of Bar Examiners on behalf of the failed applicants seeking to bring some racial diversity into the process.

For more than three years, we fought through the courts, finally arriving at the Fifth Circuit US Court of Appeals. By that time, however, several of the plaintiffs had taken the bar exam again and passed, so we lost the case.

Long after we had African Americans on the city council, in the mayor's office, and as head of the police department, blacks in our city still faced discrimination and intimidation. I was in traffic court with a client one day, and as I was getting ready to leave, I walked by the lock-up area. Inside the little room I saw an African-American man talking with a white police officer. The black man said to the policeman, "Just tell me one thing: why did you have to beat me up? You already had me. You knew you were going to lock me up. Why did you have to beat me?"

I stood there and waited for the policeman to answer, and the policeman saw me standing there, although he didn't appear to recognize me. "Because I just don't like niggers," he said.

I can't begin to tell you how hot my blood boiled. There was a time in my life when I would have invited him outside, but I have learned when to be bold and aggressive and when to lay back and take corrective action later. In this case I said nothing. Instead, I made note of the man's badge number, then left and went to

Reginald Eaves's office. Reggie was the city's public safety commissioner at the time.

"Reggie," I said, "let me tell you what I just heard."

I told him everything. He had the man summoned to his office. When the man came in, Reggie said, "I want you to meet Councilman Marvin Arrington. Mr. Arrington says he just heard you tell a guy that you didn't like blacks and that's why you beat him up. Did you say that?"

The policeman said, "Yes, sir."

Reggie fired him on the spot.

What I wanted that man to know, and every policeman in the country to know was that you can be tough, keep people in line, and still be civil about it.

More widespread than that type of abuse is the disrespect of African Americans in places of business. It is less prevalent, of course, than it was just twenty years ago, but this disrespect still exists.

I attended a convention in Las Vegas with a client, and I won a color television in a drawing they held. The set worked fine for a while, but one Saturday it broke and I wanted to get it fixed right away. So I found a TV repair shop out on Atlanta's Stewart Avenue. I put the TV in the car, and Marvin, Jr., and I drove over to drop off the set to be repaired.

I carried it in, and the man behind the counter scowled and said, "You bring a bill of sale when you come pick it up."

The man was accusing me of stealing the television just because I was black.

I said, "What are you talking about? I just want to get the thing fixed."

He said, "You don't bring a sales slip back I'm going to have your black butt locked up."

With Marvin, Jr., standing beside me and two other white men in the back of the shop, I decided that was neither the time nor the place for a confrontation. So I said, "Fine, I'll just take my set somewhere else to get it repaired."

The man said, "No, you don't understand. You don't get this set back until you bring me a bill of sale."

Now, here's what makes me furious about a situation like this. I'm an attorney, and at the time of this incident I was city council president. I could work through the system and take care of the situation, but it would be a hassle that I shouldn't have had to deal with.

But what about regular folks, good folks, who don't have my advantages? They're at the mercy of a man like this, and he knows it.

The man in the store didn't know that I was president of the city council, so I wrote a letter to Dozier Smith, the city council member for his district. I told him I had been in his neighborhood and had been treated shabbily. "Next Saturday," I said, "I'm going back for my TV set at 11 o'clock, and there's bound to be trouble if I can't take it with me. You can meet me at the store if you want to."

I sent a copy of the letter to the owner of the TV repair place, and when I got there on Saturday the man was standing there behind the counter.

"Mr. Arrington," he said, "I'm sorry. I didn't know who you were."

I said, "That's not important, who I am. You don't have the right to seize my TV or anybody's TV just because they're black. And to accuse me of stealing right in front of my son."

The man put my TV on the counter and said it was working fine. "No charge," he said, as though that would make me happy. It did not.

I am even more disappointed that my children are now beginning to experience the same type of discrimination. Just a few years ago when Marvin, Jr., was a student at the University of Virginia, I let him borrow my Ford Bronco. He and his cousin were driving to Myrtle Beach, South Carolina, on a Friday when a deputy sheriff from somewhere in South Carolina stopped him on the interstate. Marvin fit the profile—a young black man driving a nice vehicle. The deputy actually got Marvin and his friend out of the car, put them on the ground, and told them he was going to search the car. Marvin told him to go ahead, but he wouldn't find anything.

"So where do you keep the drugs?" the deputy asked.

"We don't have any drugs," Marvin said. "We don't do drugs."

"I'll find them," the deputy insisted, "so you might as well tell me where they are."

"There's nothing there," Marvin said. "We're just driving to Myrtle Beach in my father's car."

"I'll find the seeds if that's all you've left," the deputy went on. "I can nail you for that."

Marvin was mad now. "If you find seeds," he said, "then you're the one that put them there, because I don't smoke marijuana."

After lying on the ground for fifteen or twenty minutes, preparing himself mentally to spend time in jail because this guy was going to plant something, Marvin heard the deputy say, "Got it! Got it right here, boy!"

Marvin's anger raged. "You can't have anything because there's nothing in there!"

"What about this?" the deputy said, holding a six-pack of beer he had found in the storage area in the back of the Bronco.

"Must be my father's," he said, "because I didn't put any beer in the car."

"Well, you're driving the car, and I found the beer, and your license says you're not old enough to possess beer, so it looks like we're going to jail, doesn't it?"

The beer was, in fact, some I had inadvertently left sometime earlier. I called a lawyer friend of mine over there to help us out.

Of course, it wasn't the fine that bothered me most. What I hated was that my son, the next generation, was facing some of the same kinds of harassment that I had faced. When will it ever end?

It hasn't ended for me. I was driving back from Hilton Head in my Toyota Land Cruiser after a great weekend with Marilyn, Marvin, Jr., and Marvin's girlfriend. I looked in the mirror and saw the state trooper behind me. His lights weren't flashing, but I got that feeling. I looked down at my speedometer, and it was right on seventy. I had the cruise control on. I glanced back in the mirror, and said, "This guy is going to stop me."

I wasn't speeding, so I didn't bother slowing down, and a moment later his blue lights came on. I immediately pulled off the expressway and stepped out.

The troopers first words were, "Do you have a title for that car?"

"No," I said. "I just bought it last week. Here's the temporary license for it. Here's the registration and my insurance card. Here's my driver's license."

He looked at it and he said, "Okay, you can go." And that was all there was to it, but it was all so unnecessary. He had no reason to stop me and my family, except that he saw a black man driving a Land Cruiser.

Incidents like these for African Americans are more than just insulting, more than just degrading—they can be downright frightening, because even though the man you're facing wears a badge, you can't be sure what to expect.

More common, however, are the encounters with disrespect. Despite my broad political support as city council president and the good reputation I had earned as an attorney, some doors remained closed to me as an African American. One of the attorneys in the prestigious Atlanta Lawyers Club sponsored me and Judge Clarence Cooper for membership in that organization. The all-white club rejected us. The potentially embarrassing fallout from the exclusion of a superior court judge and the president of the Atlanta City Council by this private, professional organization led to a series of hastily convened meetings among the partners at various law firms. An article also appeared on the editorial page of the *Atlanta*

Constitution denouncing our exclusion. After a second vote, Cooper and I were accepted. The experience was an unpleasant reminder of the existence of people who reject you on the basis of skin color alone.

We've come a long way in my lifetime, but we still haven't created a city, a state, or a nation that treats all of its citizens equally. By almost all accounts, opportunities have greatly improved for African Americans since the days of my childhood. We obviously are much better off than we were in the 1950s. Even so, my neighbors, my family, and I still experience incidents like those described throughout this book.

I marvel at the progress we have made in race relations in a single generation. My children, Marvin and Michelle, may see a truly colorblind society in their lifetimes, but only if each of them, and their peers, accepts responsibility for creating such a society. Their actions, so far, make me optimistic.

In 1990, I witnessed one of the proudest days in the lives of dozens of Black Living Legends of Negro Baseball. Seven years earlier I had suggested that Southern Bell publish a calendar of Atlanta black history, which would serve as a living testament to the achievements of African Americans. Each year the calendar chronicles "firsts" in government, sports, education, community service, and other areas of black professional and civic life. My belief in suggesting the calendar was that young people could see models of achievement every day of the year.

As part of Southern Bell's growing commitment to African-American history, the company sponsored a reunion of the players of the Negro Baseball Leagues in Atlanta. The reunion grew into a celebration, salute, and recognition ceremony unparalleled in Negro baseball history.

Hank Aaron said of the celebration, "There are very few things I get emotional about. When I saw all of the Black Living Legends who came to Atlanta ... from all over the world ... I had tears in my eyes. Some had never been on the field inside a major league ballpark; many had been denied that 'one chance' because of the color of their skin. The reunion and recognition ceremony in Atlanta marked a long-overdue beginning, not an ending."

That beginning led to the Baseball Hall of Fame in Cooperstown, New York, the following summer, where Major League Baseball celebrated Negro League Baseball Players Day.

As a member of the boards of trustees at Emory University and Clark Atlanta University (CAU), I worked hard to direct our young people toward that day when skin color will no longer matter. In 1990, I was proud to recommend that the Emory Law School create and fund the Donald L. Hollowell Civil Rights Chair, through which the school will prepare future attorneys to ensure the rights of all citizens. As this book goes to press, I am working with the administrations of Emory and CAU to create a commission that can lead us into a new era of racial acceptance and equality.

The world I grew up in could never have conceived of such a momentous occasion. The world we have created demands it.

Chapter 4

Education

A child is a person who is born to carry out what you have started. He is going to sit where you are sitting and when you are gone, attend those things which you think are important. You may adopt all the policies you please, but how they are carried out depends on him. He will assume control of your cities, states and nations. He is going to move in and take over your churches and schools, universities and corporations ... the faith of humanity is in his hands.

—Abraham Lincoln

When I was born in Grady Hospital in 1941 and taken home by my parents to Grady Homes, African-American children living in housing projects had little hope of graduating from high school, much less college. A post-graduate degree for a black child of a truck driver and a domestic worker was almost unthinkable.

So it is a tremendous testament to my mother and father that all four of my siblings and I graduated from high school and college, and then completed our post-graduate studies. Now the grandchildren of Maggie and George Arrington are following the trails blazed by their parents and earning their professional degrees.

Because of my family's experience, I believe that all children, given appropriate guidance and instruction from their families, teachers, and communities, can achieve success.

In the words of the poet Carl Sandburg, "There is only one child in the world ... and the child's name is All Children." That said, the responsibility then falls to each of us to provide that guidance and instruction to succeeding generations. Every one of us must accept responsibility for a child or a group of young people. We may begin by spending more time with our own children, grandchildren, nieces, and nephews, taking them to plays and other events, introducing them to their cultural roots and history, going to church with them. Your sphere of influence can grow as you mentor the children of friends and neighbors, making your home a welcome haven. When our children were growing up, lunchtime for them meant lunchtime for their playmates as well. Their friends came to our home for a sandwich or whatever else Marilyn was serving. When we had extra tickets to athletic events, our children brought their friends along. These special times allowed them to see another example of a harmonious family.

The Atlanta community where I grew up challenged me at every turn to succeed both academically and as a citizen. My parents' generation invested in their children with their values, their care, their concern, their sense of humanity, and their spirituality.

Before I started first grade, my mother enrolled me in a private preschool directed by two sisters, Mrs. Scott and Mrs. Knox, in a home on Ashby Street. My mother would have preferred Oglethorpe Elementary School, a prestigious school for African-American children operated by Atlanta University as a training center for education majors. But Oglethorpe had earlier rejected my older brother, Joe, telling my mother their quota was already filled. If they rejected Joe, a straight-A student who in 1954 would earn the *Atlanta Journal* Cup for Most Outstanding Student, she knew I would have no opportunity for admission.

Mrs. Scott, through fear, intimidation and not just a few whacks with a pear tree switch, prepared me well for first grade at E. R. Carter Elementary School. That's where I became friends two years

Marvin S. Arrington, Sr.

later with Hamilton "Hamp" Holmes. But when overcrowding forced us to be transferred to English Avenue Elementary, Hamp's mother got him out of town. Maybe she thought the English Avenue neighborhood was too rough for him. For whatever reason, she sent him to Tuskegee to live with his grandmother for a few years. I didn't see him again until high school. I later met Hamp's grandmother, Mrs. Camfield, and the woman commanded respect with her mastery of the English language and her insistence on a good education for her family. I saw the importance of an encouraging family in the education process. Mrs. Camfield prepared Hamp well for the heavy load he would later carry.

The academic program at English Avenue was weaker than at Carter, and I quickly fell into the wrong crowd. I spent my time hanging out at an old stockyard company on 14th Street, wasting time and hoping for odd jobs. About that time some of my friends began to invite me to go downtown with them to shoplift. I declined. If I had gone downtown with them, my father would have beaten me to death.

I needed direction, and my fifth grade teacher, Lois Wright, found a way to instill self-confidence and direct my energy more productively. She cast me in the lead role in a school play. When I asked her whether I could handle the part, she assured me that I was bright and capable enough to take on any challenge. The play was a success.

During those years, we occasionally visited my grandfather, Idus Arrington, who had moved on to Columbus, Ohio. It was there that it dawned on me that segregation was pervasive. When the kids from Columbus would ask me if I was going back to the segregated South, I always smiled because they were attending integrated facilities, but for all practical purposes, Columbus was segregated. Most black people in Columbus spent their time on East Long or Mt. Vernon Streets, and it was like being on Hunter Street (later Martin Luther

King, Jr., Drive) or Auburn Avenue. I saw few black professionals in Columbus.

I came to understand Atlanta's uniqueness because I always saw black professionals here, and they gave me something for which to strive. Atlanta University Center is a gold mine because it produces so many black college graduates. It was understood in Atlanta that you would at least try to go to college and live a productive life.

Another school transfer took me to the brand new Alonzo F. Herndon Elementary School. I got back together with friends from E. R. Carter, started playing tennis, and had my first serious thoughts of college. Still, I remained an indifferent student as I prepared for Turner High School.

The notion of college had first entered my head when I was about seven years old. Ralph Redding, an older boy in our neighborhood, stood up to James Horn, the local bully. Although Ralph lost the fight, he became my hero for standing up to James in the first place. When Ralph later enrolled at Morehouse College, he made a great impression on me and stoked a low-burning flame of ambition in the back of my head. It is another example of the importance of role models.

In African-American schools in the late 1950s, teachers did their level best to prepare us all for college so we didn't have to remain subservient throughout our lives. Many of the older teachers had grown up in an Atlanta that offered no public high school education for African-American children—a system determined to keep them down. But they had risen to professional status despite the system, and they would lift us up as well. They pushed us hard to succeed in high school and attend college, even though segregation greatly limited job opportunities. They knew and we knew that white graduates earned more than blacks, but we were almost universally optimistic that we could break those barriers.

In my lifetime, the momentum was obvious. Since the 1920s, Booker T. Washington had been the only black high school. Then in

1947, David T. Howard, which started as a grammar school, became a high school. In the same year, Carver Vocational School opened, offering vocational training to young black people. Henry M. Turner High School opened in 1951. It may have been a sign of changing times that my high school was named after the man who had been the US Army's first black chaplain and a fiery bishop of the African Methodist Episcopal Church. Turner was a black nationalist and outspoken critic of Booker T. Washington.

My first test as an eighth-grader at Turner came not in the classroom but in the hallway. Clinton Nunnally, from the Dixie Hills section of town, stopped me on the way to my industrial arts class and demanded protection money. I quickly reviewed my options, a hungry afternoon or a fight I probably would lose. I gave him the money. Willie Battie, a friend from the neighborhood, heard what happened and pulled me aside that afternoon. Battie demanded that I uphold my manhood and our neighborhood's reputation by confronting Clinton. I knew he was right, but I wasn't ready to stand up to Clinton until Battie said, "If you don't, I'll whip you myself."

The next day Clinton found me again and tried to extort more lunch money. When I refused, Clinton pushed me. I pushed back, and then punched him several times and won the fight. Word soon spread that I was not going to be anybody's patsy. I'm still thankful to Willie Battie for reminding me of the importance of standing up for myself.

Although I had been a good student in elementary school and during the first two years of high school, I later lost interest and was a threat to become the first Arrington child not to go to college.

In high school, I began to believe that I could take care of myself and didn't need my parents, particularly my father. Shortly before Christmas the year I turned fourteen, I decided I'd had enough of school. I had gotten a little job at a downtown department store delivering packages during the Christmas holidays. I had a little money in my pocket; you couldn't tell me anything. I started cutting classes, and got kicked off of the basketball team. I figured if I couldn't play basketball, I didn't need to be hanging around school, so I dropped out—without telling Mother and Dad. Instead of getting on the bus, each morning I'd make my way to the corner of Ashby and Simpson streets to hang out with what was definitely the wrong crowd.

I figured, if worst came to worst, I could hang on the corner, shoot dice, run numbers like so many others were doing. I was definitely on the verge of derailing any possibility for future success when Raymond "Tweet" Williams, my football and basketball coach, spotted me. Coach Williams could have just called me a quitter and given up on me. He could have driven by without saying anything. How many times have we missed an opportunity to encourage a young person who needed a good word?

Coach Williams, though, did the responsible thing. He stopped and he challenged me.

"What are you doing hanging out on the corner, Bo?" he asked.

"I'm not going to school anymore," I said.

"Son, you're making the biggest mistake of your life," he said. "You need an education if you're ever going to get off this street."

I thought about what he said, and I looked around. None of my friends were with me. They were all in school. Only the older guys, most of whom had dropped out of school a few years earlier, hung out there doing nothing but running numbers and talking trash. The excitement of breaking the rules disappeared, and I was bored with the prospect of a lifetime spent at the corner of Ashby and Simpson, so I went back to school and paid the price for my delinquency.

I had been one of the few freshmen to make the varsity basketball team that year, but Coach Williams demoted me to the B-team. I might have quit the team, but I decided to stay and regain my credibility. The next year I was back on the varsity.

Friends referred to me as "Bo" long before Raymond Williams called me by my nickname. I was born with legs that have an extreme outward curvature, so I came to be known as "Bowlegs"—"Bo" for short. I may be Mr. Arrington in my corporate law practice, but to friends and family from the old neighborhood, I will always be "Bo." Seems like that name fit me better than the one on my birth certificate during those sometimes directionless years of my youth.

Then came the occasional days when I surprised my teachers, my friends, and even myself with a streak of intellectual capability and determination. One such instance came when my civics teacher, Eleanor Bradley, told the class that we all had to memorize the Gettysburg Address. Because of the significance of President Lincoln's brief remarks, I determined to fulfill my assignment. Every night for a week I read his address, then turned the page over and whispered sections back to myself.

When the appointed day came, Ms. Bradley stood at the front of the class saying we would all have to stand and recite the address. As I was walking in, she said, "Mr. Arrington, you're late, so why don't we start with you?"

I'm sure she assumed right off that I would not have completed my assignment, but would stumble through with some smart aleck remarks along the way. That's the reputation I had earned. My classmates believed the same thing. Some of them started giggling as soon as she called my name.

This time, however, I was ready. I wasn't even nervous, because nobody expected me to succeed. I stood and took my place in front of my class and began:

"*Four score and seven years ago our fathers brought forth on this continent a new nation, conceived in liberty and dedicated to the proposition that all men are created equal.*"

Immediately there came a call from the back of the room, "All right, Bo!"

I completed the address, and my classmates cheered when I finished. Ms. Bradley smiled to let me know I had done well, and then said, "You can do well when you want to."

In addition to Eleanor Bradley, who insisted that I not coast through school on extracurricular abilities alone, there was my principal, Daniel F. Davis, who refused to give up on me as a student. One spring morning I was hanging around with friends outside the main building. We had sent somebody with a car to Paschal's to get us those famous fried chicken sandwiches. This was a serious violation of the rule against leaving campus, of course. We stood around waiting and jiving, and getting more and more impatient for those sandwiches. All the while, we were oblivious to the fact that our voices were carrying through Principal Davis's open window above us. Finally, after I asked loudly, "Has he came back yet?" Davis had had enough. He came outside to confront us and delivered a scathing verbal attack, the chief point of which was our general worthlessness and lack of prospects in life. I'm convinced he was the most angered by my bad grammar.

But, the greatest impression anyone made on me during my school years was by a woman whose name I don't even remember. I was in the eleventh grade and she was a student-teacher—a Spelman College student working as an intern. She called me aside one day, away from the crowd, and said, "Marvin, you can be a good student if you concentrate on your work. You straighten out that attitude of yours and try to make something of yourself, and you can be whatever you want to be."

Others had said similar things to me, but there was just something special about the way she said it. She didn't really have any stake in that school or in me. She was just passing through, but I could see that she truly cared. And let me tell you, that woman's words stuck. I didn't become a scholar overnight, but I started taking my studies more seriously, and even thinking about where I might go to college.

Although athletics remained my first love, I addressed my studies with vigor during my senior year at Turner High School. I learned lessons both on the field and in the classroom.

I played quarterback but was not the starter at the beginning of the season. Andrew Williams was the starting quarterback, and he had the physical tools to be a great one. But he lacked something intangible—some instinct that all great leaders must have in the midst of the fight. He threw a couple of interceptions in the second game of the season, dropped the ball a time or two, and Coach Williams benched him and made me the starter.

I didn't have half the arm of Andrew Williams, and I was probably a lot slower. But we had some horses in the backfield—Bobby Thornton, Theodore Baldwin and Hamilton Holmes—and all I had to do was hand off the ball and convince the team we would win. We finished 8-1-2, and lost to Booker T. Washington in the first round of the playoffs.

To this day, I am disappointed that we could not compete against white schools in athletics. I saw athletes whom I know could have competed against the best of them, players like Buck Buchanan of Birmingham, who later became a Hall of Fame defensive lineman for the Kansas City Chiefs. Because of the small number of large black high schools, we often traveled out of town, or even out of state, to make up a full schedule, visiting Howard High School (Chattanooga, Tennessee), Parker High School (Birmingham, Alabama), Lucy Laney High School (Augusta, Georgia), Spencer High School (Columbus, Georgia), and others.

Football went a long way toward keeping me out of trouble. We had to be down at the practice field by 3:30 every afternoon, and after practicing for a couple of hours, we were too tired to start any mischief.

Being an athlete also kept me out of fights, which usually erupted between boys from different neighborhoods. Because my teammates came from all over northwest Atlanta, we put aside those rivalries and worked together to win. Even guys who didn't play football weren't going to mess with the quarterback of their school's football team.

I was co-captain of the basketball team that winter, along with Hamilton Holmes, and captain of the tennis team in the spring. Through tennis, I experienced one of my greatest lessons in humility. We traveled all the way to Durham, North Carolina, in the spring of 1958 for a tournament. I was playing the number one singles position for my school, and I drew a tall, skinny player from Virginia who had a reputation for being one of the best junior players around, black or white. I was going to prove myself against this kid.

I had a strong serve and a stronger forehand, and I decided to keep him against the baseline with my strength. I quickly realized that I had underestimated his game. That kid, Arthur Ashe, beat me like a drum—kicked my butt. He took my best stuff and did whatever he wanted to with it—put it here or there.

After the first set, which he won six-love, I said to somebody on the sidelines, "He had luck with him. No way is he going to return my serve like that again. No way he's going to hit the corners like that again."

But that's just what he did—another six-love set. He humiliated me and taught me a lesson about being gracious in victory. When it was over, he didn't gloat. He didn't laugh at the formerly cocky kid from Atlanta. He just shook my hand and prepared for his next victim. I had never planned to make my living as a professional athlete, but Arthur Ashe reinforced the need for me to focus on my studies.

Looking back, I'm not sure my mother would have allowed me, or any of her children, to forego a college education. As a girl, she dreamed of going to college herself. She made good grades in high school, and made plans to attend Paine College in Augusta, Georgia. However, her relationship with George Arrington, a young man who had come to Atlanta from Harris County, resulted in an unplanned pregnancy. My grandfather, Papa Jack, made her drop out of school and give up her dream of college.

On his deathbed, Papa Jack told my mother, "I made a mistake. A Negro without an education in this country is in bad shape."

But by then, it was too late. Mama had three children, and the best work she could find was cleaning houses for white people. Her dream then was to make sure that every one of her children graduated from college. In fact, we all earned postgraduate degrees. Her long-deferred dream was finally fulfilled—through us.

As I considered my education beyond high school, my thoughts centered on athletics. Football was the way to get a college education. I wanted to be the next Dick Calhoun, who was my neighbor and captain of the great 1951 Morris Brown College football team that beat Florida A&M and won the Southern Intercollegiate Athletic Conference (SIAC) championship.

I had precious little awareness of the great changes going on around me at the time. For example, I certainly knew that Althea Gibson had become the first black woman to win at Wimbledon and that Jackie Robinson had broken the color barrier in Major League Baseball. But I didn't know about the Summit Meeting of Negro Leaders in 1958 that called for an intensified campaign against discrimination.

While I was playing football and getting more serious about my studies my senior year, Robinson and Harry Belafonte led young people in the Youth March for Integrated Schools in Washington. Atlanta may have been quieter than other major cities during that year, but cataclysmic change was right beneath the surface. In June of 1959, we gathered in Atlanta's Municipal Auditorium in our caps and gowns. Hamilton Holmes narrated a series of readings in a portion of the commencement program that bore the title "Moments of Decision." The following months certainly proved to be so for me.

Although my mother wanted all of her children to attend college, my father suggested that I join the Navy right away. At his insistence, I met with a Navy recruiter, although I did not intend to join the military. I had no doubt that I would follow my older brother and sister into the college ranks. The only question was, where?

My first choice was Knoxville College in Tennessee. Coach Williams had helped me get a football scholarship there, and my mother had a friend who was dean of students and who might find additional financial aid for me. Even with that help, though, Knoxville would have been a financial burden on the family. I still would have to pay my living expenses, and I didn't have the money for that. So I stayed at home in Atlanta and enrolled at Clark College, partly because they offered me a football scholarship and partly because, unlike all-male Morehouse, it was co-educational.

Coach Williams, a Clark graduate, introduced me to my college coach, Leonidas Epps II, who cut an impressive figure at well over six feet tall and two hundred forty pounds. Coach Epps ran the entire athletic program at Clark, coaching football, basketball, tennis, golf, and track. I knew right off that if I got out of line, he'd jerk me right back—quickly. Still, I had to test him. It was just my way.

I didn't see the necessity of getting too serious about the early days of football practice my freshman year. Classes hadn't even started, so I didn't show up. Well, Coach Epps saw me standing outside a local pool hall and stopped.

"You're not coming to play ball with us?" he asked.

"Oh, I don't know," I said.

"Then you might be standing there the rest of your life. Come on over and try it out."

I decided to give it a couple of weeks, and I enjoyed myself.

I soon discovered that these would not be my accustomed glory days on the football field. Clark had three strong quarterback candidates in addition to me, and I spent much of my freshman year on the bench, playing substitute fullback—when I did get in. This was luck in disguise, because I concentrated on my books more than I would have as a starter.

At Clark, I found that the student who wasn't serious about his work didn't succeed. Unlike high school, the campus wasn't full of people acting the fool and, for the first time in my life, I began seeking a direction. Everybody seemed to have a purpose, and I began to recognize the difference between being a great college football player—which had been my only dream up to that point—and making a quality life for myself. I began to strive to perform well for teachers like my freshman English teacher, Mrs. Willie C. Davis, who gave me the first and only "F" I received in college. Although I flunked her class, she made me want to improve and be better.

As my commitment to learning grew, my priorities shifted from sports to academics. I knew that if I worked hard I could be a good student, but I didn't turn totally away from sports. I became captain of the Clark College tennis team, so I spent most of my spring afternoons on the courts back at Washington Park, watching a younger group come through with even more adult supervision than I had enjoyed. By that time, the city had improved the courts and made one of its wisest personnel decisions ever, hiring Branch Curington to run the center. Branch guided many boys into adulthood using the lure of tennis to keep them out of trouble. He also served as a model for adults who might make positive impressions on young people. Branch was the kind of man we need more of today in our community to encourage young people, serve as a positive role model, and provide discipline when necessary.

Several of us were playing one afternoon when a little boy (he couldn't have been older than ten) hung on the fence and watched Branch giving lessons. Tennis balls lay all over the court, and the boy eyed them, looking for an opportunity to reach in and grab one.

Branch looked over at him and said, "What are you doing, little fellow?"

"Just looking," the boy said softly. He looked like he was ready to turn and run.

"What's your name?" Branch asked.

"Horace Reid."

"Well, come in here, Horace Reid. Why don't you pick up all these tennis balls and I'll give you an ice cream cone."

The little boy didn't say anything. He just grabbed a bucket and started running around the court, filling it with balls. When he finished, he and Branch walked toward the building to get his ice cream.

"You want to play this game?" Branch asked.

"Yes sir," Horace answered.

"Then I'm going to give you a racquet, and I want to see you every morning at 10 o'clock. The first morning you miss, I'm going to hit you over the head with my racquet."

Branch sounded intimidating. If youngsters got out of line, he straightened them up in a hurry. But he was also playful, and the kids responded. Horace Reid turned out to be one of Branch's best. A few years after he walked onto the court, Horace became the first black United States Tennis Association national tennis champion from Georgia. He earned a scholarship to UCLA, and later became one of the top three hundred professional players.

Today, Horace says he owes a debt to Branch Curington and to all of the adults who encouraged him and kept him straight at Washington Park. Even the teenagers helped bring along kids like Horace. He was so good, the kids his age couldn't keep up with him. Eventually, none of us could.

I reported to football camp my sophomore year thirty-one pounds heavier than the year before and was converted to offensive guard and defensive linebacker. I applied myself to my studies that year even more than I had before.

An incident that year helped illustrate for me the importance of my education. As I mentioned, I was living at home to save money during my years at Clark. One evening as I was studying at the dining room table of our Neal Street house, two of Atlanta's small group of black policemen came to our door demanding to see Dad. They told Mother they knew he was selling moonshine and proceeded to search the house without benefit of a warrant. During the search, they passed me at the table and asked what I was doing. I explained that I was studying for my college classes. My brother and sister, who were studying in their rooms, offered the same response. Unable to find Dad or any evidence of moonshining, the police left. A few days later, these same policemen ran into my father on the street and stopped him. "We know you're selling moonshine," they said, "but we're not going to push it. If you've got three kids in college you need to be doing whatever you can to keep them there!"

Another event that shaped my path was hearing Donald Hollowell, the most prominent black attorney in Georgia, at work in a courtroom. One of my fraternity brothers was arrested for demonstrating at the Krystal restaurant in Five Points in downtown Atlanta during an early sit-in. Hollowell represented him, and I will never forget the experience of watching this polished, fiercely intelligent black man standing before a white judge, eloquently arguing points of law.

I was never arrested for demonstrating, partly thanks to Coach Epps and his insistence that his football players confine their civil protesting to the off-season. He encouraged us to attend rallies and conferences at all times of the year, but to stay far away from any activities that could land us in jail and keep us off the field.

There were other reasons for avoiding protest, of course. Authorities often published lists of "agitators" which were sent to the hometown newspapers of out of town students. Their parents were then at great risk of being fired by racist employers. Student membership in suspect organizations could also be risky. Professor James Green, who taught American history at Clark, insisted that all his students become members of the NAACP, but he had all our membership materials sent to him at the college. That way students could not be traced back to their local communities and their parents not targeted for reprisal.

During this time of renewed academic focus and awakening social consciousness, I was still the rough-and-ready football player. My competitiveness was well known. During one game with South Carolina State, I came in to replace Lowell Dickerson. Lowell whispered to me to watch out for the opposing lineman. On the next play, that lineman knocked me out cold with a forearm. I was revived with smelling salts and woke up swearing and demanding a chance to get the guy who had hit me with a pipe, but I was too dizzy to get back into the game.

I'm happy to say we won that game 28-6, which was not an unusual point spread for the highest scoring team in Clark's history up to that time. That same year we upset Fort Valley State College 14-0, shut out Alabama State, Tuskegee Institute, and Savannah State, and beat Morris Brown 34-14. The sour note of the season was our 21-12 loss to Morehouse.

Off the field, the faculty at Clark was instrumental in exposing us to events in the outside world, bringing a host of dynamic speakers to campus to challenge both the status quo and our hearts and minds. Malcolm X came to speak at the invitation of Professor C. Eric Lincoln, author of *The Black Muslims in America*. The faculty was also attentive to our exposure to the arts, bringing Ruby Dee and Ossie Davis to Clark. In the same year the Negro Ensemble Company performed *Death of a Salesman*, and made a tremendous impression on me. As I watched Willie Loman sit in his apartment and talk about all the things he was going to do, knowing he was never going to do them, I saw distinctly the difference between rhetoric and execution. I had always been a person of action, and after seeing *Death of a Salesman*, I knew I would have to act in a well-considered manner in order to achieve success.

I was a much better student, but I still needed additional direction. The professors and administrators at Clark, outstanding scholars such as Dr. James P. Brawley, Alfred Spriggs, J. J. Dennis, Dean Alphonso A. McPheeters, Averett Burress, Willie C. Davis, and Stella Brooks kept me on course.

I could have completed college in the spring of 1963, but because the football team was headed for a particularly strong season that I didn't want to miss, I made no effort to complete my graduation requirements. I returned in the fall for one more season.

My instincts about the team were right on the money, and in the fall of 1963, we had a superb season. We whipped Fort Valley State 42-0, trounced Tuskegee 67-0, and humbled Alabama State 60-0. The sweetest of all were our victories against both Morris Brown and Morehouse. At the end of that season, I doubted I would ever accomplish anything as great as that season with the Panthers.

I graduated from Clark shortly after the season ended and worked for eight months, saving money for law school, which I began in the fall of 1964.

Preparing for Law School

Howard University was the first choice for many of us considering careers in the law. Howard had the distinction of being a virtual training camp for civil rights attorneys, and its faculty had included lawyers like Thurgood Marshall, who argued successfully *Brown v. Board of Education* (Topeka, Kansas) and became solicitor general of the United States before becoming an associate justice on the US Supreme Court. Other faculty members were Herbert O. Reid, who had won many precedent-setting cases; Patricia Harris; and Dorsey Lane, for whom fellow Atlantan Vernon Jordan had served as a student assistant. I concluded that Howard University was the place to be.

Jerome Shuman, James Sheffield, and "Chick" Chisholm were also there. The dean was Clyde Ferguson, who had just left Harvard Law School to work at Howard.

I also considered the law school at North Carolina College at Durham, where I was offered a scholarship. I asked my friend Clarence Cooper to join me there, but Clarence had a scholarship to Howard and was excited about the opportunities there. Then my brother Joe, who was in dental school at Howard, urged me to apply to that great institution. Joe told me, "You have several black law schools—Florida A&M, North Carolina College, Lincoln University, Southern University, South Carolina State, Howard University—but the cream of the crop is Howard. If you're going to law school, go to the best you can get into." He knew that without the scholarship I would have had at North Carolina, money would be tight, so he invited me to live with him and his wife for five dollars a week.

With their persuasion, I enrolled at Howard, and with my $1200 in savings, I headed to Washington with Clarence Cooper feeling like something of a crusader, preparing myself to uplift the community with my talents. We truly were caught up in the social movement and had little concern for ourselves. We had an opportunity to correct injustices—to create a more open society. Earl Hilliard, a Morehouse graduate, rode the same train with us to Howard. On that long trip to Washington, I told Cooper over and over, "We can't fail. We've got to make sure we come back as law school graduates."

Even as we prepared to leave for school in the hot summer of 1964, race relations in the United States had deteriorated greatly. A major civil rights bill had been passed, but there were racial insurrections all over the Northeast. Like a brush fire, they jumped from New York's Harlem and Bedford-Stuyvesant across the Hudson to North Jersey. In Rochester, the National Guard was called out. That same summer, three civil rights workers were murdered and buried with a bulldozer in Mississippi.

Cooper, George Edgecomb, James Felder, Robert Travis, and I—all Clark graduates—joined the largest freshman class in the history of Howard. Until then, Howard had averaged fifty or sixty students a year, but with the need for civil rights lawyers all across the country, especially in the rural South, they accepted 150 students my first year. From our class would come many outstanding leaders of the next generation. Cooper became a federal court judge; Edgecomb a superior court judge in Tampa before his death from cancer at age thirty-one; Earl Hilliard, a congressman from Alabama; George Brown, a member of the Tennessee Supreme Court; Ralph Cook, a member of the Alabama Supreme Court; James Felder, a member of the honor guard at President Kennedy's funeral and later a member of the South Carolina House of Representatives; and James Long, a superior court judge in Sacramento, California.

I learned quickly that law school was much tougher than college. Most of us were soon putting in twelve- and thirteen-hour days of class work and study. Cooper and I, who had become acquainted at Clark, studied together and visited often during that first year. It was a difficult time and friendships became lifelong bonds.

After several months, the pace began to wear me down. In addition, I ran into money troubles. By December, much of my savings had been spent on tuition and living expenses.

My friend and classmate, Jimmy Porter, who was always in good spirits, sometimes saw me looking particularly downcast, and always said, "Keep getting up, Bo! You've got to keep getting up!"

I knew my money had to last through spring, so I lived as if I were broke every day, eating Spam for lunch and a TV dinner for supper. A fraternity brother who had graduated from Morehouse ahead of me, Jim Hudson, was working in Washington and fed me once or twice a week. Jim drove a Triumph TR4, and I loved to hear that little car drive up. One positive financial note actually came from the segregationist Georgia government. The state to which my mother and father and I had paid taxes all of our working lives wanted so badly to keep African Americans out of its universities that it paid me to go to a school outside of its system. So every semester I used my state of Georgia check to help pay for tuition.

Thinking about Returning to Atlanta

But it wasn't enough. In midwinter, cold, discouraged and homesick, I called Mama and told her I was ready to sit out a year and earn enough money to come back. She said, "Baby, if you drop out now, you're never going to go back." Five days later, when I picked up my mail I found a box with a chocolate cake and a check for five dollars from her.

One day during spring semester, my high school classmate, teammate, and friend, Hamilton Holmes, knocked on my door. Hamp, who along with another Turner classmate, Charlayne Hunter, had endured vicious racially motivated attacks to integrate the University of Georgia, was now a medical student at Emory University. He stopped in Washington on his way back to Georgia from a visit up north.

When I told him about my first year at Howard and how much I missed Atlanta, he said, "Why don't you transfer to Emory, Bo?"

Emory Law School had no black students, but Hamp was sure the school was ready to integrate. I filed the information in the back of my mind, but made no plans to enroll at Emory. I would return to Howard in the fall.

Cooper and I went back to Atlanta the summer after our first year of law school to work in the post office, a job that Fifth District Congressman Charles Weltner had helped us secure. After one day back home, I knew I never wanted to leave Atlanta again. I loved my hometown. And yet, what other choice did I have?

I considered Hamilton Holmes's suggestion that I enroll at Emory Law School. As the summer drew to a close, and with another year in Washington facing me if I didn't make something happen, I put on my best suit, got into my Mama's car, and drove to Emory University, a few miles east of downtown Atlanta.

At that time, Dr. Sanford S. Atwood was heading the entire enterprise at Emory, and he represented a significant departure from tradition. Atwood was a Presbyterian from the North who came to Emory from Cornell. His presence suggested that the Old South character of the school was about to change. While on the surface it might have appeared that Emory's Lamar School of Law was still doing what it had done best for years—namely, to polish the skills of young white college graduates for careers in the lucrative areas of corporate, real estate, and tax law—Dean Ben F. Johnson was quietly orchestrating his own revolution. Dean Johnson also served in the Georgia State Senate, and many would later point to the opening of a new law school at Georgia State University as his greatest accomplishment. But his contributions were much greater in the areas of social and institutional change.

Dean Johnson recruited a cadre of assertive young faculty members to supplement the veterans. At the same time, he devised a strategy to increase the number of black law students. One major obstacle to his plan was the fact that black students often did not score well on the standardized Law School Admission Test. Johnson also realized how prohibitive the cost of a private law school would be to many black students.

While at a conference of the American Association of Law Schools in Chicago, Johnson and Michael DeVito, one of his young faculty members, attended a seminar about racial bias in the LSAT. When he got back to Atlanta, Johnson formulated a plan, which led to a five-year grant from the Field Foundation in New York. The plan called for the recruitment of black college graduates for a summer session of courses at Emory. Students would be selected primarily on the strength of recommendations from their undergraduate advisers. Emory's resources, combined with the grant from the Field Foundation, paid the students' tuition and provided a stipend to offset the loss of their summer earnings. Those students who completed the three classes with an average of seventy or better would be admitted to the law school and given financial support for the first year.

Johnson believed that the LSAT was culturally biased and was thus a poor predictor of success for black students. For the purpose of testing his hypothesis, but not as an admissions requirement, he had all the black students take the LSAT before they entered Emory and after they completed law school. Johnson also instituted a blind grading system to protect against any intentional or unintentional bias. The first "Pre-Start" program, directed by Michael DeVito and advised by Dr. Melvin D. Kennedy of Morehouse, began in the summer of 1965 with twelve black students. As it turned out, Dean Johnson proved his point at the end of the experiment. Eleven of the first twelve students successfully completed their summer work and enrolled in the law school, and this pattern continued in subsequent summers.

Of course, I knew none of this the afternoon I parked Mama's car on campus and made my way to the law school building. All I knew was that mine was the only black face in sight.

I went into the building with its facade of Georgia marble and elegant central staircase and began to study the bulletin board to calm myself. An older gentleman stopped and asked if he could help me. I told him I was a student at Howard Law School. He introduced himself as Dean Johnson and invited me into his office.

We had a constructive conversation, in which he got out of me that my grade average at Howard was seventy-six. Within a few minutes, he asked me if I would consider coming to Emory. Suddenly my casual exploration was turning into a major route change. Having secured my admission to Emory in about fifteen minutes, I headed for Clarence Cooper's house to tell him the news. Cooper found it hard to believe. As we sat in Cooper's kitchen, I got right to the business of convincing him to come with me. I had not only sold

Dean Johnson on me, I had told him about Cooper, too. "Look, man," I told Cooper. "I don't want to go there with all those white folk by myself. You gotta come, too."

Cooper was not interested at first. He liked Howard and the cosmopolitan atmosphere of Washington. But his mother was listening to us talk, and she chimed in and said, "Marvin was good enough to tell the dean about you. At least go out and talk with him."

So Cooper agreed to visit Emory with me. Dean Johnson conducted a gracious interview and satisfied himself that Cooper would do well. Then, as he had done with me, he leaned forward and asked, "Would you transfer to Emory?"

Cooper started throwing up obstacles as fast as he could. His transcript wasn't available. "No problem," Dean Johnson said. He could register him before it arrived. Then he said he didn't think Emory would give him credit for his full year at Howard. Dean Johnson assured him they would. Soon Cooper was out of concerns, and he and I were scheduled to be the first black, full-time students at Emory School of Law.

Our enrollment at Emory would soon have a more far-reaching effect on other African-American college and professional students. The old Georgia statute requiring the state to assist with the cost of my education, originally intended to "encourage" black students to enroll at out-of-state schools instead of seeking admission to state institutions, included language that was just fuzzy enough to qualify Cooper and me for subsidy at Emory. All we had to do was sign a waiver that we would not attend the University of Georgia and two-thirds of our tuition was paid for.

Dean Johnson had to sign the documentation, and he was incensed by this law. In his role as a state senator, he moved in the subsequent legislative session to ensure that the statute was stricken. By then, though, I had used my check to buy a run-down Renault to get me back and forth to school.

Cooper and I were both excited about our first day on campus. Dean Johnson made it clear to us that we would be welcomed, and we expected nothing less. It was the fall of 1965, and schools all over the South were integrating peacefully. Plus, we were enrolling in law school, where students expect a higher degree of professionalism.

I picked up Cooper in my Renault for our first day of class, and we were heading out Ponce de Leon Avenue when that old car broke down. So instead of making a historic entrance to the law school, we stood in the middle of the street with the hood up trying to determine the problem. We laughed at the racial stereotypes our lateness would confirm for some, but it would take a few days for us to truly enjoy the humor in the situation. We arrived on campus at around noon, having missed the first two classes of the day, and it seemed like the whole student body was standing outside to witness our great entrance.

I have very good memories about the way Cooper and I were received at Emory. Nobody ever let the air out of my tires. I don't recall anybody ever using the N-word. People knew the time had come. Our first day on campus, Ben Shapiro, another student, introduced himself and invited me to have lunch with him the next day. I was apprehensive but accepted his offer. Ben and I have now been friends for more than three decades.

Soon Cooper and I were just two more would-be lawyers buried in the grueling routine of law school. Besides, our appearance on campus was no news event in comparison to the controversy swirling around an October issue of *Time* which asked, "Is God Dead?" and identified Thomas J. J. Altizer of Emory's religion department as one of the radical theologians who would answer the question in the affirmative. We were small potatoes compared to that storm.

Almost everybody bent over backward to help us succeed. Cooper has said that although we didn't have much in common with the other students, my ability to play tennis served as something of an icebreaker. I remember few unpleasant, race-related incidents during my two years as a student. Occasionally a student in the library would move to another table if I sat in a chair next to him, and Cooper reminds me of another time when a professor belittled my reasoning in class. Cooper says he took it personally and was convinced his hostility was racially motivated, but I don't remember the incident. Perhaps my glasses are rose colored when I recall those years.

Those first days at Emory and our warm reception would begin for me a life-long relationship with the university, culminating in my service on the Emory Board of Trustees. I had the good fortune at Emory to take an evening course in litigation from Lloyd Whitaker, who became my friend and sometimes fierce competitor. His course was informal and he encouraged us to trust our instincts on human nature. Whitaker portrayed the courtroom as a stage for the improvisational theater. The attorney, he said, was the playwright, producer, director and one of the lead actors, and the jury's verdict provided the ultimate critical review.

My style in those days often was to speak before I thought. At the same time, Whitaker recognized good instincts and my penchant for hard work. I would take his direction to heart and spend my career honing those instincts and tempering my quick tongue.

After classes, Cooper and I often went over to Donald Hollowell's law office on Hunter Street, where we found a warm welcome. We always valued the opportunity to use the law library of our role model, and drew inspiration from being in Hollowell's presence. This was the man who counseled Martin Luther King, Jr., the man who represented Charlayne Hunter and Hamilton Holmes when they knocked down the doors at the University of Georgia and opened the way for African Americans to attend any public college or university in the state of Georgia. Donald Hollowell was the man who won battle after battle in courtrooms with his understanding of the law and his quiet but firm demeanor. He stood as the finest example a young lawyer could follow, and I learned everything I could from him. Never in my wildest dreams would I have imagined that he and I would someday be law partners.

I also got into the habit of going to the law school library on Friday nights when most people were taking a break from the books. I could work better when the library was nearly empty and very quiet.

In my last two years at Emory, I clerked for two of Hollowell's partners who later became judges: Horace Ward (now a United States District Court judge) and William Alexander (a Fulton County Superior Court judge). These men exuded knowledge and wisdom, and even then I could foresee the opportunities opening for them to serve a higher calling. To help me earn some money, Horace let me teach his business law class at Atlanta University. Living at home and earning a little money here and there left me much better off financially at Emory than I had been at Howard.

While at Emory, I also experienced my first taste of politics by working on the campaign to re-elect Charles Weltner to Congress. Weltner had gained national attention as a political emblem of the new, moderate South.

While I burned the midnight oil, the world outside Emory shook with further political and social unrest. Racial disturbances took place in the Midwest and even in Atlanta's Summerhill neighborhood where I was born. Congress ousted Adam Clayton Powell, Jr., as chairman of the House Education and Welfare Committee. In Georgia, the legislature attempted to keep Julian Bond, who had been duly elected to that body, from taking his seat because of his support of Student Nonviolent Coordinating Committee's anti-Vietnam War stance.

Vietnam was beginning to supplant the civil rights movement on the front pages of the nation's newspapers. Martin Luther King, Jr., insisted that the conduct of the war and the repression of blacks were philosophically related. In a case that would later touch me directly, the World Boxing Association and the New York State Athletic Commission underscored King's point when they took away

Muhammad Ali's championship title after he refused induction into the military because he was a Muslim minister.

Keeping the Commitment

I graduated from Emory in the spring of 1967 with all of the Arringtons in attendance. Finding work as a fresh law school graduate was no easy task. I signed on as a law clerk with a flamboyant black attorney and state senator, Leroy Johnson, for the princely sum of seventy-five dollars a week.

I guess you can say I began fulfilling my obligation to help those who followed me shortly after I graduated from Clark College, when I taught Sunday School at Lindsay Street Baptist Church. I had grown up in that church, listening to the Reverend H. M. Alexander preach from the pulpit, and I wanted to give something back. I volunteered to teach a class of young people.

I was no Bible scholar, so I spent a good bit of time preparing every week. Most of my lessons focused on the importance of staying in school and earning a degree. I don't know what specific impact I had on the kids coming through, but several of them later went on to college. Two became medical doctors and another earned a Ph.D.

Of course, in most cases, we must start much earlier preparing children for the future. Any improvement in the education of our children must include more than just bricks and mortar. On a visit to Detroit in 1994, I witnessed an innovative program that seemed to be working there. I shared what I'd seen with the Atlanta school board and the police department, and both agreed on an initiative to allow Atlanta police officers to volunteer to read to students in elementary and middle schools. During their off hours, the officers read stories with contemporary themes that addressed social values such as responsibility, honesty, cooperation, and peer pressure.

We called the effort the Reading Patrol, and we identified five goals for its success: preventing crime, decreasing the student dropout rate, increasing reading skills, reducing disciplinary problems in schools, and enhancing the relationship between police officers and youths.

Our law firm took a more direct role by participating in the Adopt-A-School program. We adopted Grove Park Elementary School and persuaded Atlanta Gas Light Company to adopt E. R. Carter Elementary School, where I attended first through third grades. Prior to the school's closing by the Atlanta Board of Education, Atlanta Gas Light provided money for a student honors recognition program, financed an end-of-the-year luncheon for the school staff, and established a program in which company employees joined kids at the school for lunch each week for one-on-one mentoring.

In 1986, with the assistance of Southern Bell, I organized the Visions of Excellence Program, which brings high school juniors and seniors to an all-day seminar to discuss issues of critical concern to them. The program deals with issues such as the status of the black family, substance abuse, teenage pregnancy, economic development, and violence. The response was so positive, the Reverend Jesse Jackson, head of Operation PUSH and former presidential candidate, served as the keynote speaker the second year of the program. Visions of Excellence continues to serve young people and draw nationally recognized leaders as motivational speakers.

In addition to these and other programs, my active participation in educational institutions continued when my alma maters, Clark Atlanta University and Emory University, invited me to serve on their respective boards of trustees. My service to the schools has been a tremendous honor for me, as well as a great responsibility. In 1987, I was called on to help make one of the most significant changes in Clark's history. Craig Beverly, a professor at Atlanta University, shared with me a position paper calling for the merger of Clark and Atlanta University. Atlanta University was just beginning to recover from a crippling financial crisis. Clark was operating with a balanced budget, but enrollment was shrinking.

"Marvin, both of these institutions are going to fail if they don't consolidate, cut their expenses, and move forward," Beverly explained. "Would you be willing to submit it to the Board of Trustees at Clark?"

"Sounds reasonable and interesting," I said. "We'll look into it."

A committee was created with trustees from Clark and Atlanta University to explore the possibilities.

The two schools complemented each other beautifully. Atlanta University had physical facilities and a graduate school that would greatly enhance Clark's programs, and Clark offered financial stability that AU needed at the time.

The boards of trustees agreed to the merger and asked me to put together the necessary legal documents. In addition to the more public opportunities to serve, my assistance to Clark Atlanta University (CAU) and Emory has included considerable behind-the-scenes discussion and advice. For example, I spearheaded the establishment of the L. S. Epps Athletic Scholarship Fund at Clark in honor of our great coach and athletic director. The fund benefits students with demonstrated financial needs and is funded by the generosity of former Clark College and Clark Atlanta University athletes.

Of course, education is closest to my heart when I talk about my own children, Marvin and Michelle. When Marvin was growing up, we talked often about what college he would attend. He had the ability and the opportunity to go to a prestigious university, and I encouraged him to take that path. At the same time, though, we discussed the tremendous benefits of a smaller, historically African-American school like Clark Atlanta University, where I believe students in that more intimate setting get the added attention they might need to succeed.

Marvin decided to attend the University of Virginia, where he excelled. Then he earned his law degree at Emory University. He joined my law firm for approximately two years after which he left the firm and started his own practice.

Michelle earned her undergraduate degree from Howard University, and on May 8, 1999, Marilyn and I sat among the proud parents to watch our daughter receive her diploma. The commencement ceremony was as moving as any I have ever experienced. I came to understand the importance of Howard University in a new, personal way. Even as a law student at Howard, I had not fully appreciated the great richness of the institution.

At the 1999 ceremony, University President H. Patrick Swygert presented honorary doctorate degrees to U. N. Secretary General Kofi A. Annan, who gave the commencement address, and to Olympic gold medal winner Jackie Joyner-Kersee. An honorary doctorate was also awarded posthumously to Kwame Ture, also known as Stokely Carmichael.

In his remarks to the graduates, President Swygert reminded them of the many great leaders who had preceded them: doctors, engineers, lawyers, business people, and statesmen. He mentioned several exceptional graduates by name: Thurgood Marshall, Vernon Jordon, Andy Young, Gabrielle McDonald (chief judicial officer of the World Court), Debbie Allen, and Phylicia Rashad. As the president spoke, I was deeply moved. Then, he said that the class of 1999 has its own great leaders, who will be the leaders of the future, and he mentioned Michelle Arrington specifically.

With that, Marilyn and I were brought to tears.

Chapter 5

Getting the Job Done

Ask my friend Lowell Dickerson to describe me, and the first thing he will say is, "Marvin Arrington has always had a job."

He's right. At various times in my life, I delivered produce, delivered newspapers, delivered packages for Davison's Department Store (now Macy's), picked tobacco, worked as a janitor, and waited tables at The Piedmont Driving Club, The Jewish Progressive Club, and aboard a train traveling across the western United States. I did whatever it took to put a dollar in my pocket and stay out of trouble. I had no choice, for segregation had as one of its centerpieces miserable wages for African Americans. We had to overcome this deliberate economic discrimination by working long and hard hours.

My mother and father provided the model of hard-working parents committed to providing the necessities for their children, although we almost never had anything more than just the necessities. If I wanted anything extra, I bought it with my own money.

My grandfather, "Papa Jack" Andrews, first showed me how to earn a dollar. I was seven or eight years old when I rode with him in his International pickup truck, selling produce door-to-door through the Buckhead community.

Then I went to work, "throwing" the *Atlanta Journal* for K. C. Marks, the district distribution manager, and a model for anyone willing to work hard to make a living. K. C. had little formal education, but he owned eight or ten rental houses, so he had plenty of money. Yet he never showed off. He wore overalls every day, and in that low-key, hard-working way, he took care of his family. I threw newspapers all the way into my years at Clark College.

The summer before my senior year in high school, I got a taste of the kind of work I could be doing the rest of my life if I didn't get a decent education. My brother told me about a job picking tobacco up in Connecticut. He had done it himself the previous summer, and he told me I could make good money. My first thought was that my great-great-great-grandparents, Moses and Hattie Hitchcock, had picked plenty of tobacco and cotton as slaves down on the farm in Baldwin County a hundred years earlier. I didn't need to revert to that kind of job, but then somebody said that Connecticut is much cooler than Georgia in the middle of summer, and the cool breeze blows across the fields so that you hardly break a sweat.

A bunch of guys went up from Atlanta every year, they said, and I ought to go, too. I took the bait and found myself on a train to New York with a hundred or more college guys. As I talked with some of them, I soon became suspicious. I couldn't find many of them who had worked this job the summer before. You would have thought if it was such a great job more would have signed up for seconds.

After a day and a night on the train, we climbed out somewhere in northern New York state, and then loaded into several buses headed into Connecticut. The buses stopped in a little town called Melhurst and let us off. As we unloaded, the first thing the man in charge did was take our return tickets. "We don't want you to lose them," he said. I nervously handed over mine, wondering what would happen if I decided tobacco picking wasn't for me.

It didn't take until noon the next day to realize I had made a big mistake. Most of the guys around me agreed. They put us out in a field that was covered with huge tents, which apparently enhanced the quality of Connecticut Valley tobacco, then told us to get down on our butts under the tents and start picking tobacco. Anybody could see right off that if there were any breeze to be had, it wouldn't be under a tent.

Our job was to strip two or three lower leaves from each stalk, a process they called "priming." We had to be careful not to bruise the leaves as we pulled them off since they would be used whole to wrap cigars. Then we had to string them up so they would dry slowly. When we finished working one field, we would move to another one. By midday the first day, those big tents had become like ovens. It must have been 120 degrees under there, and we were already discussing mutiny. I said if I ever had children they would never have to do that type of work. I'm sure Moses and Hattie Hitchcock hoped the same thing for their children, but the message was lost across the generations.

We awoke one morning, after we'd been there for a couple of weeks, and twenty-five or thirty guys had disappeared. Somebody had broken into the safe where they kept the train tickets, and those fellows got out of there. The rest of us stuck it out, and I made about three hundred dollars for my work. When we finally got back to Georgia, we all were at least twenty pounds lighter than when we left. Bob Jones, who would later become my brother-in-law, was so thin his mother cried when she saw him.

I swore I would never be a field hand again, and I rededicated myself to the goal of a college education.

I left the South again in the summer after my freshman year at Clark, and this time it was a much more pleasant experience than picking tobacco. Some of the older waiters I worked with at the Jewish Progressive Club and the Piedmont Driving Club talked often and fondly of their experiences working as railroad dining car waiters out West. I decided to apply for a summer job with the Union Pacific Railroad, and received a quick reply telling me that if I could get to St. Louis, they would put me on a train to Ogden, Utah. I followed my instructions and arrived in Ogden a few days later. There I bought a white shirt, black pants, and bow tie to match the white jacket I wore to work. The routes took me to St. Louis, Los Angeles, Las Vegas, or up to Idaho. I saw all kinds of people: rich and poor, prostitutes, gamblers, and alcoholics. Most of my customers tipped well. I must have made fifteen hundred or two thousand dollars that summer.

One day I was waiting on a white man who asked where I was from. When I told him, he said, "Small world. I'm from Cartersville."

We talked for several minutes, and then I moved on and took care of some other people. When I came back by his table again, we talked pleasantly for another minute or two. The headwaiter, who was white, came up about that time and joined the conversation. Then, while I stood there, the man from Cartersville told my boss, "If this boy gets out of line, let me tell you what we do with them down South. We whip their butts."

I felt like he'd hit me over the back of the head with a two-by-four. I thought, "What got into him, talking like he wanted to be my friend, asking my name and where was I from one minute, and coming out with that the next?" I turned around and walked away. I knew then and there I had to finish college and not wait tables the rest of my life. My work schedule that summer positioned me perfectly to prepare for another year at Clark.

I traveled on the railroad three or four days a week, and I had assumed when I left Atlanta that everything out West was integrated in the early 1960s—that only the South remained segregated. Las Vegas was one of several cities along the line, however, that remained segregated. In Las Vegas, the black waiters had to stay in private homes while our white counterparts stayed in hotels. In fact, African Americans could not visit any of the casinos in downtown Las Vegas; our entertainment was restricted to the black neighborhood. I had assumed up to that point that whenever I left the South I would no longer have to deal with segregation. But when I followed the call to "Go West, young man," I learned that the West wasn't so different from the South.

In Ogden, the railroad put me up in the Royal Hotel for five dollars a week, and I spent most of my time in that quiet community of Mormons, thirty-five miles north of Salt Lake City. I often walked to Webber Junior College (now Webber State University), three miles from my room, and read books and magazines and newspapers from across the country. Because of the failing grade Mrs. Davis had given me in freshman English, I worked particularly hard on my writing skills. I bought a little book entitled, *How to Write*, and I read that book and worked through the exercises three or four times that summer. Years later, after I passed the Georgia Bar examination, Mrs. Davis would kid me that I never could have done it without her. She probably was right. Had she not flunked me in that one course, I might never have buckled down and developed my writing skills.

The next summer, I stayed in Atlanta and took a job as a janitor at the Ford Motor Company plant in Hapeville, one of the first companies in town to integrate. That job gave me firsthand experience of how some white people enjoyed intimidating black people.

Every day I heard taunts and epithets. In the bathroom men had posted announcements for Ku Klux Klan meetings or had written threatening graffiti. There was always talk about putting sugar in the gas tanks of black workers so their cars would stall. I don't know if that ever happened to anyone, but I felt the threat every day. I felt the eyes watching me, and I wondered what might happen if I found myself in the wrong place alone with the wrong man.

I completed my studies at Clark College in January 1964, and the opportunities for employment for black people had not improved significantly. For me and many other black college graduates in the early 1960s, law was beginning to look like the best option for people interested in social change. People like Donald Hollowell, Thurgood Marshall, and Vernon Jordan were held in high esteem in our communities. Many of my friends were becoming social workers, moving to New York, and earning ten thousand dollars a year. That was more money than most of them ever could have hoped to make in the South. The chance to make good money and help other people at the same time intrigued me. For several years, however, I had considered attending law school, and I knew if I took a couple of years off now I would probably get married, have a baby, and never go back to school. So I decided to enroll in law school.

I did have a few months in the working world, however, because I had stayed at Clark an extra quarter. I could not begin classes in law school, wherever I decided to attend, until the following September. So I got a job with the P. Lorillard Corporation, selling cigarettes. My job was to drive all over the city and make sure all the stores had our brands, Kent and Newport, displayed prominently. They gave me a company car and paid me seventy-five dollars a week, and in my mind I was doing as well as any young black man in Atlanta.

Of course, we all still dealt with segregation on a daily basis. DeKalb County, in those days, had earned for itself a rough reputation among African Americans. Sometime after downtown Atlanta restaurants began serving blacks, I went with several white colleagues to Evans restaurant, a few blocks from Emory University. We were met at the door by the manager, who looked at me and said, "This guy cannot come in here to eat." The anti-segregation laws were already on the books, so, legally, he had to serve me, but there I stood, one black among forty or fifty whites, and the time did not seem right to challenge the man.

In my work with Lorillard, I had developed relationships with store managers who made merchandising decisions. At the end of each week I reported to a man named Don Williams, who worked out of the first floor of the Darlington Apartments on Peachtree Street. One week, I turned in my report to Williams, and in it I said, "Kent and Newport are doing well."

He brought the report out from his office and said, "We need to make a correction, Arrington."

"What's that?" I asked.

"You've made a mistake in your grammar. Let's change it to Kent and Newport is doing well."

I never had quite gotten over the "F" I received from Mrs. Davis, so I immediately re-read the sentence. Upon thorough examination, however, I knew absolutely that I had written the sentence properly.

"You change one word," I said, "and you'll be making a mistake. The grammar is correct as written."

"We'll see about that," Williams said, and he stuck the report under the nose of his secretary, who was at her desk nearby. "Read this and tell us whether Arrington has written it correctly."

The woman read the sentence and laid the report on the side of her desk. She didn't look up.

"Well?" Williams asked.

"Well, what?" she replied almost silently. She clearly did not want to step into the middle of this one.

"Well, who's right?"

"He is," she said without looking up.

Williams stared at his secretary, stunned, then snatched the paper off her desk, stomped into his office and slammed the door. Even after Williams left the room, she still wouldn't raise her head. In her mind, aligning herself with me could cost her her job or worse. Still, that did not stop her from telling the truth, and I never forgot her little act of courage.

A few days later, I submitted my resignation, giving notice as I had learned in college. "Mr. Williams," I said, "I'm enrolling in law school, and I want to give you two weeks' notice."

"Law school!" he said. "You'll never make it in law school."

"Oh, yes I will. You don't have the right to pre-judge me."

"Well, then, you get yourself on out of here today," he said. "I don't need you hanging around here if you're leaving in two weeks anyway."

"I wanted to work my notice," I said, "give you time to find a replacement. Plus, I was trying to save as much money as I could before I went off to school."

"Well, you won't be getting any more from me," he said.

He took the keys to the company car and I rode a bus home.

That might have been the end of the story, except that I saw Williams years later walking on Marietta Street down near the Henry Grady statue. He was walking kind of stooped over and had a mean and cold look about him. Life had not been good to him. I lifted a hand and spoke.

He looked at me good and said, "Do I know you?"

"Oh, you know me, Mr. Williams," I said, "from a long time ago. I just thought I would say hello."

Then I was back on my way.

Chapter 6

The Law

There are thousands of stories like ours out there. The difference is in how people dealt with it. Marvin prepared himself for a better future—college, law school. He persevered. And he never denied his early beginnings, when people spit on him. How could he? Those were defining moments.

—Lonnie King

When it's appropriate, Marvin's style is to go for the jugular. His style is something that people either like or dislike.

—Senator Leroy Johnson

One of the greatest feelings in the world for me is to go into the courtroom as a warrior, prepared to defend or to seek appropriate redress for wrongs inflicted upon my client. My clients place their lives in my hands when we enter the courtroom together, and I do not take that responsibility lightly. I fight to win.

At the same time, I defend the system and the Constitution of the United States. I learned from Don Hollowell, Leroy Johnson, Howard Moore, Jr., and Horace Ward that you prepare well and you give it your best shot. Unfortunately, when your client's fate is placed in the hands of the jury, you don't always win. But, victory is not always measured in wins and losses.

When I graduated from Emory Law School in 1967, recruiters for Atlanta's major law firms had no interest in black applicants. Our opportunity to learn and grow came from the dozen or so black lawyers who maintained practices in the city.

Leroy Johnson opened his door to me. I went to work with Leroy at his office on Gordon Street. If any man has both style and substance, it's Leroy Johnson, Georgia's first black member of the General Assembly since Reconstruction. He was elected to the state senate in 1962. While he made a tremendous impact during his years in the legislature, his most lasting contribution might be the leadership he provided young black lawyers.

He quickly became my mentor and one of my closest advisers, and remains so today. He also provided examples of commitment in law practice and in his politics. For example, in the state senate, he sometimes committed to vote a certain way and, prior to the vote, realized that he was making a mistake.

"If I give my word to vote for it," Leroy would say later, "I voted for it, even if I have to hold my nose and raise my hand. The only way around that commitment is to go to the person to whom I had committed my support well before the day of the vote to give him time to replace mine with another. I believe it's a sin to give a commitment and then fail to keep it without sufficient prior notice."

That type of loyalty earned Leroy tremendous respect in the Senate, in his law office, and in the community. In fact, the *New York Times* once said he was "by any standards, the single most powerful black politician in Dixie. In his uncanny ability to deliver huge blocs of votes to the candidates of his choice,"[1] the *Times* continued, "in his shrewd political horse-trading designed to benefit black Georgians and—not incidentally—himself, and in his often brazen pragmatism through which he converts political enemies into expedient, if temporary, friends, Leroy Johnson is without peer in Southern black politics."

---

[1] Stephen Lesher, "Leroy Johnson Outslicks Mister Charlie," *New York Times Magazine*, 8 November 1970, 34–54.

Leroy fascinated me in his ability to deliver votes on the state senate floor. If, for example, a senator from Macon wouldn't commit to a bill Leroy believed was important, he'd get on the phone and call fifteen or twenty black folks down in Macon and tell them what was up. The next day the furious senator would find Leroy and demand, "What do you mean having all those people calling me last night?" Leroy would respond calmly, "I just need your vote, Senator."

And he would get it. Leroy stayed so cool, never answering his colleagues' anger with anger. He didn't have to. He had the power.

In my experience, Leroy Johnson was the original velvet hammer, and although my style doesn't always reflect it, I learned a tremendous amount from him.

"Sometimes you must merge your style with your objectives," he'd say when we were sitting around at the end of a long day. "I believe you can catch more flies with honey than with flypaper, whereas you, Marvin, are often more forceful. You must be willing to make occasional compromises to achieve your goals."

While this is true, the time comes when you have to take off the gloves. Sometimes you have to push and push and push for your principles, or they'll be lost. Those of us who were students in the '50s and '60s believed in pushing.

And yet, Leroy Johnson knew when the time came to fight.

He often quoted Dr. Benjamin E. Mays, president of Morehouse when Leroy was a student: "Get yourself an ideal and cling to it and cleave to it as though it was God Almighty, because in order to survive in a segregated society, you must be iron clad and steel girded."

I greatly admired Leroy Johnson's political style, but was lukewarm about a political career for myself. At his request, I worked on the campaign of Jack Etheridge for a Fulton County Superior Court judgeship. Leroy, however, supported his opponent, attorney Ralph McClellen. One day when I was fed up with the gritty machinations behind the scenes, I exclaimed to Johnson, "I don't like politics. I'll never get into it." Johnson smiled and replied, "Never say never!"

While working with Leroy, I learned that even a law degree did not immunize a black man from racial harassment. An especially bigoted clerk at the courthouse was infamous for his hostility toward the small number of black attorneys who came to his office. He had no real power, so he took malicious delight in stamping the documents we submitted and then literally throwing them back at us.

Others had let this behavior slide, but I'm not the type to accept a personal affront. The first time the man hurled papers at me, I went back to Johnson's office and reported the problem. I still don't know what Leroy said or did, but the next time I went to the courthouse that man treated me like a gentleman.

Working in Johnson's office was invaluable experience, but when my father died from a stroke in 1968, I moved back home and started looking for a better paying job so I could relieve the financial burdens on my mother. My search led me to John Dean, a Howard graduate and a Phi Beta Kappa, who headed up the regional headquarters of the federal Office of Economic Opportunity in Atlanta. John signed me up as a South Carolina field representative working out of Atlanta at a salary of twelve thousand dollars per year.

It was an exciting time to be part of Lyndon Johnson's War on Poverty and to help direct the resources of the federal government toward long-delayed educational and social improvements. My duties took me from the Black Bottom of Columbia to Orangeburg to Walterboro and into more rural areas of the state. On Dafuskie Island, I had the privilege of helping to establish the first Head Start program. It was also part of my job to monitor new health care programs. There was great satisfaction in using the muscle of tax dollars to demand and get better treatment for black children.

At OEO, we knew we were on a mission to help others and make a difference in their lives. We taught people to read and to work with their hands. My role was to evaluate programs. I also used my official position to push for the elimination of racially segregated waiting rooms in health care facilities.

I also had my first run-in with the FBI. It would be nine more years before the National Association of Human Rights Workers would publish its lengthy document titled *The Dilemma of Black Politics: A Report on Harassment of Black Elected Officials*, but already the evidence was mounting that black politicians were being singled out for harassment, including Adam Clayton Powell in New York, Mayor Carl Stokes in Ohio, and others.

Although I had little power in my position with OEO—especially as compared to a congressman and a mayor—I gained firsthand experience with the harassment they encountered. As part of my job, I had recommended the awarding of a human services contract to an organization directed by several former student leaders of the civil rights movement. I filed my report in Atlanta on a Sunday afternoon, just before leaving town for South Carolina on assignment. The contract went through on Monday morning.

A few weekends later, an FBI agent appeared at my front door grilling me about the contract. I knew that the issue wasn't the contract itself. Somebody just didn't want those former student leaders to get the government work. While I was giving guarded answers to the agent's questions, the phone rang. On the line was a friend telling me that he had heard the FBI was on the way to my house. The warning may have been late, but the information was helpful. My friend went on to tell me that the agent would try to trip me up about the fact that the contract was awarded on a Monday when I wasn't in town. I went back to the living room and the agent asked me to sign a statement. Of course, I refused to sign anything without the benefit of review by my attorney, and the disgruntled agent went away. I never heard from the FBI about the matter again.

I left OEO and became student personnel adviser at Emory University while I prepared for the Georgia Bar Examination. After I passed the bar, I made plans to leave Emory and begin my law practice. Robert Herman, a law school classmate, invited me to join his firm of Kleiner, Herman, Deville & Simmons, and I accepted. As a general practice lawyer, I took anything I could find—real estate transactions, divorce cases, wills, and lots of criminal defense work. I'd make myself known in the courthouse, in neighborhood bars, on street corners, and in church. One day, somebody pointed out that many of the large, "respected" firms wouldn't take on "common criminals." The only kind of crime they touched was "white collar." I said, "So what's so special about a man who puts on a white shirt before he robs you?"

My business grew faster as an associate than anyone expected—so fast that, after I had been with the firm for just eighteen months, I asked that they make me a partner. They conceded my point, making me the first black partner of a downtown white law firm in Atlanta. With a greater sense of ownership, I pushed even harder to build the practice. And I loved it, especially the courtroom.

Many of my clients came from the Neal Street neighborhood, people like Ace Johnson, Jr. Ace had been a few years behind me at Turner High and was working at the Atlanta Water Works when he bought himself a Cadillac with leather seats. The police reasoned that he must be selling drugs to afford such a vehicle and, after investigating, made an arrest. Ace called me to defend him.

It was one of those cases a defense attorney loves, where I knew something the prosecutor didn't, something I knew would blow the case wide open, if my timing was right—something right out of television's Perry Mason or Matlock. Except in this case, I didn't find it through investigation. It dropped right into my lap.

The prosecution's star witness was one of Ace's alleged associates, James "Mule" Clark, a man I recognized from the neighborhood. When I saw Clark approach the witness stand, I scanned the witness list for his name and didn't see it.

The bailiff swore him in and the prosecutor asked, "State your name."

Clark gave another name, and I was stunned. He appeared to be lying about his own name. I might have stepped up right then and pointed out the apparent perjury, but I was not obliged to. I let him tell his story, which painted an awful picture of Ace.

When my turn came to cross examine him, I asked if he remembered swearing to tell the truth. He said he did.

Then I asked again, "Do you recall swearing to tell the truth while your hand rested on the Bible, that most sacred book?" He said he did.

I let the silence lie for a moment so he could think about what he had said and what I might know. Then I asked the judge to admonish the witness about the severe penalties attached to perjury. I turned and faced a perplexed prosecutor and tried to control my glee while the judge explained the consequences of lying in court.

Then I turned back to the witness and, with my sternest scowl, said, "Now, with that in mind, please tell the court your real name."

"James Clark," he said.

With his truthful answer on the record, I rested my case. In my closing argument, I explained to the jury that the state's key witness even lied about his own name. How could they accept the validity of the rest of his testimony? The jury quickly acquitted the defendant.

In another case allowing me to turn the tables on the prosecution, an older man named Bobby Moore called one day and said he had been arrested for possession of illegal whiskey. When I looked into Bobby's case, I couldn't believe anybody had probable cause to search his garage. Agents of the Georgia Bureau of Alcohol and Tobacco had secured their search warrant on the grounds that they could smell the odor of white liquor coming from Moore's garage. I wasn't about to let them get away with that. When the case came to trial, I pressed the agent who had testified to having such fine olfactory capacities. He pushed back just as hard, testifying after his many years of experience, he could smell illegal liquor "from twenty miles away."

I turned quickly away from him to avoid laughing in his face, because that was just the statement I was hoping for. The night before, I had gone to a house in my old neighborhood and bought a half gallon of moonshine. I reached behind the table and brought out that bottle of crystal clear liquid. The agent knew immediately what I was doing, and so did everybody else in the courtroom. Every eye was on the government man to see if he would squirm.

I held onto the moment as long as I could, then said, "So tell me, then, is this a bottle of whiskey or water?"

The agent said he couldn't be sure.

"Thank you," I said. "That will be all."

In those days, I was chasing for work wherever I could find it, and I was happy to accept appointments from the courts to represent clients who couldn't pay for attorneys. Being on the appointed list in 1972 resulted in my being introduced to another level of criminal defense when Roger T. Eley became my client.

Many considered Eley to be one of the South's most notorious criminals, with alleged ties to organized crime in other parts of the country. When the authorities arrested him on charges of bank robbery in 1972, he chose not to retain private counsel. US Magistrate Judge J. Roger Thompson appointed me to represent him. I suspect that Judge Thompson selected me in order to give Eley a judicial slap in the face. He had a good idea what Eley's response to a black attorney would be. When I got to the prison in Jackson, Georgia, for my first meeting with my client, Eley greeted me with, "I don't want a nigger representing me." But he had no choice since Judge Thompson was not going to replace me.

I didn't know the extent of the case the government planned to present against Eley, so I filed a lengthy pre-trial discovery motion in US District Court, which requested a list of materials in the prosecution's possession. This was a standard type of motion that criminal defense attorneys often filed, only to see them denied. To my amazement, Judge Newell Edenfield issued a fifteen-page order that required the government to release to me not only the names and addresses of its witnesses and a synopsis of their testimony to the grand jury, but a wealth of other information as well. When the prosecutor's attempts to overturn the order failed, the government dropped the case. This so-called Eley Motion established a precedent in the Atlanta judicial circuit.

Eley was now delighted with his "nigger" lawyer. Two weeks after his release, he showed up in my office to ask for my continued services. Other major criminal cases began to find their way to me, and Eley himself did his best to keep me busy. The next year he was arrested again, this time for allegedly taking part in a plan to smuggle two tons of marijuana into the Norfolk, Virginia, airport. He had been picked up by law enforcement officers when he showed up at the warehouse to which the marijuana was shipped. They couldn't connect him directly to the contraband, but they suspected that he had sensed a trap when he got to the warehouse and that he had swallowed the claim check.

To represent Eley in Virginia as an attorney from out of town, I needed local counsel to sit in with me. I was always interested in promoting black attorneys, so I wrote to the chief judge of the court in Norfolk and asked him to supply me with information about black attorneys in the area who were good at criminal defense work. The judge replied that he did not normally refer lawyers to one another, but he would make an exception due to the nature of my request. One of the names he suggested was attorney William T. "Billy" Robinson. I immediately recognized the name. Robinson had been a student at Morehouse while I was at Clark, and he graduated from Harvard Law School. His wife, Sylvia, and I had grown up together. Billy agreed to team up with me in my representation of Eley. I had done all the preparation, so Billy's role was simply to sit with me at the defense table and give me access to the Virginia courtroom. I laughed and said, "I'm going to show a Morehouse man how to try a case."

This time, the case against Eley depended on the testimony of another inmate. The witness claimed that Eley, after he was put in prison, had told him all about the incident at the warehouse. He said Eley had indeed swallowed the claim check. But we managed to show that this inmate was a weak link in the prosecution's chain because he was, in fact, in love with Eley's beautiful wife, Sandra.

When Sandra Eley would visit her husband in prison, the inmate-turned-witness always tried to make contact with her. That failing, he began to write love letters to her. We suggested to the jury that his motivation for testifying against Eley was his infatuation with Sandra Eley. We succeeded in damaging the inmate as a witness and securing an acquittal for Eley. But the government was not finished with Roger Eley. Not long after the Norfolk trial, federal officers arrested him when he stepped off a plane in Atlanta. They charged him with failing to respond to a criminal subpoena to appear before a grand jury in another case. Eugene Medori, a classmate of mine from Emory, launched a strong prosecution.

This time, I built my case around the contention that Eley had been receiving threatening phone calls that put him in fear for his life if he agreed to testify publicly. Our case was strong enough to keep the jury from reaching a verdict, and the judge declared a mistrial. In the second trial, the judge ruled that I could not use the same defense. There was nothing I could do but challenge the prosecution about procedural points, and this time the jury found Eley guilty. Despite this conviction, Eley wrote me a letter of appreciation.

Still, I had not seen the last of him. Federal authorities had arrested Forrest Roberts, an Eastern Airlines pilot, for negotiating the sale of drugs that he had allegedly conspired to smuggle into the country. This was one of the largest drug busts in Georgia history. Eley recommended that Roberts hire me to defend him. Ed Marger and Nancy Lawler were also representing Roberts and his codefendant, Thomas Ruck. During the prosecution's case, we learned from an undercover agent's testimony that a government informant had assisted with the investigation. Marger asked if the informant had actually been a party to the sale of the illegal drugs. To our surprise, the agent, Gene Matthews, replied that he had indeed been involved. He also volunteered the information that the informant had handed money to one of the co-defendants during the transaction.

Under the law, the name of any informant who participated in a criminal act had to be revealed. Marger then requested the person's name, but the witness refused to divulge it. During the course of the trial, Eley had been calling me almost daily to ask how things were going. I soon became very suspicious about his level of interest in the case.

Agent Matthews asked the judge to let him confer with me privately in the witness room. My colleagues were shocked that the government's chief witness would ask to see the lead defense attorney out of the presence of everyone else. The judge granted the unusual request, and Matthews and I left the courtroom. Matthews urged me not to press our request for the informant's name. He stressed that it would greatly hamper the government's ongoing investigation if the name became public. Then he hinted that I would be very surprised if I heard the name.

"You know where I'm headed," he said.

"I don't want to hear it," I answered. It didn't take a Phi Beta Kappa to figure out that he was referring to Eley, but I didn't need to hear that from Matthews. I later learned of rumors that the government had persuaded Eley to give damaging information in the case by threatening him with another lengthy prison term. Eley and I never discussed the matter, and I still don't know absolutely who the informant was.

Matthews and I returned to the courtroom, and we continued our demand for the name of the informant. Since the prosecution would not give us the name, the judge had no choice but to dismiss the charges.

By the mid-1970s, the demands of my law practice and my service on the city council took so much of my time, I'm not sure my marriage could have survived the pace for many more years. That's about the time I met a young lawyer named S. Richard Rubin, who reminded me of where family belongs in my list of priorities—at the top. Dick and I met for the first time in the coffee shop on the second floor of the Fulton County Courthouse. I don't remember who spoke first, but we quickly began to talk business and compare cases.

Dick had moved to Atlanta in 1969, and sometime before he and I met, the Bar Association asked him to identify lawyers who would volunteer their services for kids who needed legal help. Many of these teenagers had left home, for whatever reasons, and were hanging out or living around Peachtree Street, between Tenth and Fourteenth Streets. Those blocks were the closest thing Atlanta had to a "hippie district." Police officers patrolling for drug arrests didn't have to look hard to find them. Dick got involved in a lot of Fourth Amendment work, protecting rights against unreasonable searches and seizures and ensuring that police had probable cause before hauling kids off to jail.

What these kids were running into, in terms of being overwhelmed by the police and judicial system, was nothing new to black people, young and old. Every day, somebody called me and said they had been arrested—when all they had been doing was hanging out on the corner.

As Dick and I got to know each other, we realized we held the same philosophical values, so we started working together on some cases. About the same time, I hungered for a stronger professional leadership role than was possible for me at Kleiner, Herman, Deville, Simmons & Arrington. Dick, also, was open to a new arrangement, so we created a partnership, Arrington & Rubin. I believe ours was the first black-white equal law partnership in Atlanta, and I never enjoyed practicing my profession more. Back then, the practice of law wasn't as technical or as complicated as it is today. We didn't have any staff, so we didn't worry about overhead and personnel problems. We recorded our fees on yellow legal pads. We spent all of our energy fighting the system and defending our clients, primarily in criminal court.

Dick and I brought distinctly different client bases to the partnership, a key to financial success in the legal profession. Dick also brought a long-range management style to the practice that I would value and eventually adopt professionally, personally, and politically. Dick insisted that everyone associated with our firm should build up some security, and he set about implementing insurance and retirement programs.

He also insisted that we get out of the office and spend more time with our families, and we found that our families enjoyed each other's company as much as Dick and I did. Marilyn and Dick's wife, Suzanne, were both schoolteachers. Our children were close in age, and our families fit well together for the dozen or so years of Arrington & Rubin. In the courtroom, we made a great team. One of our first and most difficult cases came when a middle-age white woman sought our help. Her son, a student at George High School, had been charged with the murder of a black teenager from the same school. The woman clearly was not wealthy. We knew that we might lose money on the case, and that defending a white boy who had killed an African-American student might cost us politically, but when the mother described the circumstances around the killing, I believed her son was not guilty of murder.

"They tell me you can save my son," the woman said.

How could we walk away from that? Dick and I took the case.

In the courtroom, witnesses testified that two teenagers had run up to our client's pickup truck in the school parking lot and demanded money. Our client tried to push his attackers from the cab, but they persisted. That's when our client pulled a knife and stabbed one of his attackers in the throat. The boy bled to death.

Dick and I argued before Judge Luther Alverson for a directed verdict of justifiable homicide. A directed verdict is almost unheard of. It means that the defense doesn't have to put up a case—that the prosecution's case is so weak, the judge sees no reason for the trial to go further. Judge Alverson agreed with our argument and set our client free. Dick and I were pleased with the outcome, but we couldn't help wondering if we would have been as successful if our client had been black and the victim white.

Of course, we successfully defended many black clients as well. For example, when a gang of hoodlums crashed a party in a Perry Homes apartment and terrorized the guests, the host pulled out a gun and demanded that they leave. They refused, and even dared the man to use it. He did, and was charged with murder. Then he called me to defend him.

Before the jury, I insisted upon my client's right to defend his home, and the twelve agreed. They found the man not guilty of murder, but guilty of simple battery.

Arrington & Rubin was earning a reputation as a firm that knew how to kick some butt in the courtroom. In time, people outside of Georgia began calling us for help. A woman from Florida came to Atlanta to ask us to represent her son, Lloyd Sealy, who was charged with murder. Sealy was a US serviceman who had completed a tour of duty in Vietnam. After going home to Tuskegee, Alabama, he contracted gonorrhea from his wife. The prosecution alleged that Sealy's response had been swift. According to the government's case, he raced to Atlanta to purchase a .38 caliber revolver. He then returned to Alabama and fired six shots into the head of his apparently unfaithful wife as she sat on the front porch of their apartment.

When we arrived in Macon County, Dick and I found that much had changed since the days when men like Arthur Shores and Donald

Hollowell were defending black clients in small southern towns. We knew that the population of Macon County was overwhelmingly black, but we were not fully prepared for the appearance of a black judge. Back home we still argued before an all-white court. In this case, an all-black jury pool ruled out any strategies involving challenging jurors on the basis of race.

But our confidence swelled when the special prosecutor from Phenix City, Alabama, wearing a shabby suit and a shirt with coffee stains, stood to begin his presentation of the state's case.

"We're going to have a field day with this guy," I whispered to Rubin.

The man's appearance, I quickly realized, had deceived us. He turned and faced the defense table and I saw his Phi Beta Kappa key and I said, "Hold on, Rubin, we're about to be in trouble."

The prosecutor argued eloquently against our client, and soon the big city lawyers were in trouble. By the end of the trial, he had worn me out. I had nightmares for three years about how badly he had shown us up. He took an empty chair and put it over by the witness stand and said, "Oh, if Mrs. Sealy could only be with us now to tell us what really happened. If she were here, I can tell you what she would testify." He gave us a lesson in litigation that I will take to my grave. Our defense of Sealy, which focused on the immorality of his wife as sufficient provocation and offered temporary insanity as justification, did not hold up against the state's evidence. The jury found Sealy guilty. We were somewhat comforted by that fact that our defense of Sealy probably influenced the judge to sentence him to only ten years in prison. But Sealy's mother did not believe we'd done her son any good at all. She rushed up to us after the verdict, crying hysterically and claiming that her son had not received justice.

I called upon the wisdom of Herbert O. Reid, my professor at Howard Law School, who gave this measure of victory: If you're facing the electric chair and you get life, that's a victory. If you're facing life and you get twenty years, that's a victory. If you're facing twenty years and you get five, that's a victory.

I tried to explain to Sealy's mother the measure of victory we had achieved. Her son might have gotten life in prison instead of ten years. But there was no convincing her that the light sentence was some degree of success. We returned to our Atlanta law practice much wiser about assumptions and first impressions.

During that period of my legal career I was also learning that the behavior of individual judges did not always measure up to the prestige of their high offices. One Fulton County Superior Court judge was disdainful of protocol and enjoyed receiving pleas in private chambers. In this off-the-record setting, he felt free to regale captive lawyers with his often bigoted stories and opinions. One day as several of us stood around his desk, he made a decidedly anti-Semitic remark.

Without really thinking, I declared, "I don't play that s---, your honor."

I realized immediately that my language had been inappropriate, but I had to make my point. "If I let you get away with that," I continued, "the next thing we know you'll be telling 'nigger' jokes when I get out of the room. No, sir. We're not going to play that way."

From then on, at least in my presence, the judge kept his personal prejudices to himself.

A confrontation with another judge cost me dearly. I had two cases to come up on the Fulton County Superior Court trial calendar at the same time, one before Judge Clarence Cooper and one before Judge Ralph Hicks. When I reported to Judge Cooper's courtroom, I was ordered to proceed to trial. I had picked a jury and was in the process of questioning my first witness when the sheriff's deputies came into the courtroom and said that Judge Hicks had ordered me to come to his courtroom and start trying the other case immediately.

I apprised Judge Cooper of the situation, and he said that I was already on trial and I must proceed. Judge Hicks thereafter terminated my relationship with my client in his courtroom, and I had to return a substantial fee to the client.

It was unfair for one judge to order a lawyer to his courtroom knowing full well that I was on trial, and then make me return a fee. Judge Hicks could have selected another case from his calendar to move forward and allow me to complete the case in Judge Cooper's courtroom. I felt I had been mistreated in a way that I would not have been had I not been black.

Perhaps the most celebrated case in which I was involved during my partnership with Dick Rubin was the defense of Arthur Langford, Jr., who served for years as an Atlanta City councilman and was a founder of the United Youth Adult Conference, a community outreach organization aimed at helping black youngsters and their families.

I remain convinced that Arthur was the target of a concerted effort to harass and discredit black elected officials. It was one of the high points of my legal career to help prove to the world, not only Arthur Langford's innocence, but his value to our community

A native Atlantan, he decided as a teenager to commit himself to public service. As student government vice president at Price High School, he introduced Dr. Martin Luther King, Jr., at a school assembly in 1965, and was moved by the remarks of Atlanta's own Nobel laureate. After Dr. King's assassination, Arthur wrote a play, *Life of a King*, and he performed the lead role many times in the ensuing years. While a student at Morris Brown, he helped fulfill Dr. King's dream in real life, working with the Southern Christian Leadership Conference to register and educate voters across the South.

Then, four years to the month after Dr. King's assassination, Arthur was shot, although not fatally, in the midst of what thousands of African Americans believed to be a crystallizing point in the community. He was among many in the community protesting in support of striking employees in front of Holy Family Hospital on the evening of April 27, 1972. Theirs was a valiant cause.

Holy Family Hospital had been established by the Catholic Medical Mission Sisters in 1964 as an integrated facility—the first hospital in the Southeast to allow black and white physicians to practice as peers. In those days, of course, integrated health care was not welcomed by the white community. As the *Atlanta Journal* reported in a 1972 analysis, "Some southwest Atlanta whites said the Catholics were building a 'nigger hospital.' The hospital stood by its policy, even as those [whites] who shouted did so over their shoulder as they sold their homes to blacks and fled with more than deliberate speed to suburbia."[2]

By 1972, the Holy Family patient population and the hospital staff both totaled more than 90 percent African American, replacing once white majorities, but the hospital's board of directors was still predominantly white, and the hospital director, Lee Nichols, was white as well.

So when Nichols fired a dozen or so black employees for attempting to form a union, Hosea Williams, a community activist and one of Dr. King's former lieutenants, led a protest that lasted almost three months. At times, more than a thousand supporters of the fired workers picketed the hospital. Then Hosea, Arthur, and two others embarked upon a hunger strike to increase the pressure. The hospital responded by turning away new patients and sending many of those in beds at Holy Family to other hospitals.

Andrew Young, then on Atlanta's Community Relations Commission, negotiated with the two sides for a settlement, but hospital management appeared ready to close the facility rather than allow a union vote. They blamed their decision on the protesters.

------

[2] *Atlanta Journal and Constitution*, 30 April 1972, 2-A.

"Hosea can take that coffin and bury the hospital about the time he starves to death," one hospital trustee was quoted in the *Atlanta Journal*.[3]

Senator Leroy Johnson donated a tent to house the hunger strikers. That tent sat in front of the hospital and became a focal point of the raging debate.

Then the management's hard-line response took a bizarre twist. On the night of April 27, shots were fired into the tent from a passing car. A bullet hit Arthur. Another hit fellow protester, Willie Ricks.

Arthur recalled the details later: "At first, I thought it was just a car backfiring. And then I saw the blood on Ricks. It was the next bullet that hit me. Ricks didn't care that much about prayer or anything else. On the way to the hospital Ricks asked me how I was doing, and I said, 'Ricks, I think this is it,' because I could look down and see a big hole here next to my heart. Ricks put his hand on me and said for the first time, 'Say a little prayer for me, too.'"

A deeply religious man, Arthur Langford prayed often. When he recovered from the shooting, he was back on the picket line three days later. Several days after the shooting, Atlanta police arrested Lee Nichols, the hospital administrator, for shooting Langford and Ricks. This professional man was accused of a drive-by shooting. The city was stunned by his arrest.

But we learned just how much race mattered in 1972 at the Fulton County Superior Court. A white man with a mountain of evidence stacked against him could still avoid conviction.

When Nichols went to trial, his lawyers succeeded in seating an all-white jury, but there were still witnesses who were present at the event. Nichols's bodyguard, whom he had hired in the midst of the hospital controversy, and the hospital controller, had been in the car with Nichols when the shots were fired. Nichols was in the back seat.

---

[3] Ibid.

The bodyguard, who had driven the car, testified, "I heard shots go off, turned around, and saw Mr. Nichols holding a gun."

The hospital controller testified that he took the gun from Nichols and removed several spent shells from it.

Then Nichols took the stand and denied before the jury that he had fired the gun. His attorneys built their defense around the tension surrounding the hospital during the protests.

The jury deliberated less than two hours, then came back and acquitted Nichols. *Acquitted* him!

The southwest Atlanta community, of course, was livid. The good news, though, was that a larger positive issue had emerged from the protests and the shooting. Andy Young successfully negotiated an end to the dispute: the fired workers were rehired, and employees were allowed to vote whether to unionize. And, more than ever, the African-American community felt a sense of ownership in the hospital. The hospital was deeded over to the southwest Atlanta community and was renamed Southwest Community Hospital.

Shortly thereafter, Arthur Langford announced his candidacy for city council. He was only twenty-three years old, and no man that young had ever been elected to a seat on that body, yet Arthur won the post in 1973 with a campaign budget of just $2,800. As a fellow councilman, I watched him immediately go to work for his district, helping to bring economic development and recreation facilities to areas around Collier Heights, Bankhead Courts, and Perry Homes.

Outside the council, he always had young people in mind, serving as Youth Director at the Butler Street YMCA and working as assistant to the pastor of Free for All Baptist Church. He also organized the United Youth Adult Conference (UYAC) to help find jobs for young people. Some of those jobs were at the Southeastern Fair, on the Lakewood Fairgrounds, in the fall of 1978.

For several years, the FBI had been looking into the affairs of the Southeastern Fair, following up on allegations about the extortion of promoters by the fair's management. Arthur called me when he learned that the FBI had extended the scope of its investigation to include him, and that his case would be coming before the grand jury.

I still don't understand why the feds targeted him, but they pushed, and pushed hard. Remaining true to the pattern we see repeated so often, they based their case on the testimony of a witness who had run afoul of the law.

Fred Williams, convicted in the 1950s on narcotics charges, robbery, and armed robbery, worked for Arthur's UYAC in 1978. When Don Pavel, promoter of the Southeastern Fair, told Arthur he suspected Williams of skimming some of the UYAC money, Arthur followed up on the charge and decided to replace Williams. Soon thereafter, Williams accused Arthur of extortion and bribery and offered to become an FBI Informant, for which he received a $1,000 fee and later an $800 monthly stipend when he was placed in the US Witness Protection Program. The government's entire case hinged on the allegations of this disgruntled former employee.

Arthur Langford, Jr., had not yet achieved great influence and power, although he was well on his way. Then came Fred Williams, and before Williams was through, he would have the FBI casting its nets all over the place trying to catch somebody—anybody.

He came to my office with Arthur to meet with me and Tony Axam, another attorney who was working on the case at that time. The first thing Williams asked was whether he would be protected by attorney-client privilege. I told him he wasn't my client, so no such privilege existed between us. Then he asked us what we wanted him to say to the grand jury—what story did we want him to tell?

I explained to him that I have never encouraged a client or a witness to lie, and never would do so.

As it turned out, Williams had a microphone in his shoe and the FBI recorded our conversation. What they got on tape was my voice urging Arthur Langford and Fred Williams to tell the truth or, if necessary, to use their Fifth Amendment privilege to remain silent.

They heard me tell Arthur that if he were honest, the evidence would show that the government had "been misinformed by its informant."

FBI Special Agent William Whitley later testified that he had expected one of us to tell Williams to lie to the federal grand jury. In other words, they were coming after anybody they could get—Arthur, Tony, or me. I felt bad at that point that I had brought Tony into the case.

When I learned that my own government had targeted me in such an underhanded way, I was incensed. First of all, why would the FBI assume that Arthur Langford would ask Fred Williams to lie? Even more disturbing, why would they think that Tony or I, officers of the court, would risk our careers by encouraging a witness or a client to lie? But what really set me off was that they would invade an attorney-client conference—the most sacrosanct confidential relationship—with a microphone and recorder. We immediately filed motions against the FBI and the federal prosecutor, charging unethical and illegal conduct. The court ruled against us and the case moved toward trial before US District Court Judge Newell Edenfield.

The government's case against Arthur was built around the following circumstances:

In September 1978, Arthur entered an agreement for UYAC to supply a grounds crew and ticket takers at the Southeastern Fair. The Fair would pay $15,000 to UYAC, including a $3,000 donation to the organization, in two installments during the fair's two-week run.

On the day the fair opened its gates, promoter Don Pavel told Arthur that he wouldn't be able to pay the fee as initially agreed. As an alternative he offered to meet the UYAC payroll on a daily basis. He said he still would make the $3,000 donation. Arthur appointed Fred Williams to supervise the UYAC staff and to receive and disburse pay.

When Pavel accused Williams of skimming from the payroll money, Arthur fired Williams immediately. In retribution, Williams made his own accusations. He went to the FBI and claimed that he had received $2,000 from Pavel to deliver to Arthur as a bribe. In return, Williams claimed, Arthur was to use his influence as a councilman to help Pavel deal with city agencies. The night before Arthur was indicted, Williams, in Judas-like fashion, invited Arthur to his home for dinner.

The prosecutor brought Arthur before a federal grand jury, where Arthur explained he never received any money from Pavel. All of it had gone to pay his young employees. Arthur was later charged with perjury because the money, technically, had passed through his hands when he used it to pay his employees. The government insisted, therefore, that he had "received" it even though he had immediately disbursed it.

Two of our law partners, Jack Goger and David Walbert, joined Dick Rubin and me in defending Arthur. They, too, were convinced that the charges were part of a broader plan to discredit black elected officials.

Our pretrial motions, in addition to claiming prosecutorial misconduct, attempted to impeach Fred Williams as a witness by raising his criminal record. In a bizarre twist, that motion led to charges of criminal contempt against me and my partners. Joel M. Feldman, the federal magistrate appointed to hear pretrial motions, referred to an unrecorded side-bar conference in which he claimed to have ruled that we could not refer to any of Williams's convictions that were more than ten years old. Facing potential fines or jail time, now we felt harassed.

There clearly was no basis for the contempt charge, which Judge Edenfield later summarily dismissed.

Jury selection for Arthur's trial began, and when we looked at the pool of potential jurors, we saw only two black faces. The prosecutors struck them immediately. We made our opening arguments and the prosecution began presenting its case. During the lunch break on the second day of the trial, several of the jurors were in the courthouse snack bar. Elsewhere in the federal courthouse, prosecutors handed down an indictment against Bert Lance (former US budget director during the Jimmy Carter administration.) When a reporter shouted into a telephone near the snack bar, "Lance has been indicted!" one of the jurors remarked, "All politicians are crooks."

An off-duty police officer reported the remark to me, and I asked Judge Edenfield to investigate. The judge concluded that the incident was true and that the jury's decision-making process would be contaminated by that juror's opinion. He declared a mistrial.

A month later we started all over. Again the prosecution systematically sought to strike every black juror from the pool. We moved to have the charges against Arthur dropped because of this clear violation of his right to have a trial by a jury of his peers, but Judge Edenfield rejected our motion.

As proceedings finally began, tragedy struck. Dick Rubin's mother, who was visiting him for a couple of weeks, walked with us up Marietta Street toward the federal courthouse as we discussed what we expected from the prosecution. Along the way, she began breathing hard and stopped to take some medicine, insisting she would be all right. She wanted to see her son's partners "in action."

But she never got to see us work. In the middle of jury selection, she suffered a heart attack in the courtroom. Paramedics rushed her to Grady Memorial Hospital, where she died. Judge Edenfield postponed testimony for one day, but we wanted more time. The death of a friend always reminds us to put things in the right perspective—to reexamine our priorities. But we also had responsibility for the life of another friend, and if the judge said the system wouldn't stop for a couple of days to grieve with us, then we had to prepare and move on.

Don Pavel, the fair's promoter, did not testify, claiming to be incapacitated by terminal cancer. The government's case, therefore, rested almost solely on Fred Williams's testimony and tape recordings he had obtained. In addition to the conference in our office, Williams had taped several other conversations with Arthur.

We responded aggressively, first by convincing Judge Edenfield to allow disclosure of Williams's criminal record. Then, instead of sidestepping allegedly damaging evidence on the tapes, we put Arthur on the stand to respond to it. For many hours the jury, each member wearing a set of headphones, listened as we replayed the recordings, stopping the machine after each potentially damaging statement for Arthur to offer his explanation of it.

The jury began deliberating, and for two days we paced the halls of the federal courthouse waiting, rushing in each time the jury announced a verdict on a charge. At 5:00 P.M. on the first day, the jury declared Arthur innocent of extortion. The courtroom erupted with applause from supporters. An hour later, the jury came in again and said they had found Arthur innocent of charge that he had asked Fred Williams to lie on his behalf.

The final charge, perjury, proved more difficult for the jury. Twice, on the second day of deliberation, they asked the judge, "Does he have to have the intention to lie?"

"Yes, I would have to say he does," Judge Edenfield replied.

When the jury sent a message to the judge that it could not reach a consensus on the perjury charge, the judge's first response was to direct a mistrial on that count. We protested, and I convinced the judge to recharge the jury by reading to it a special instruction on perjury and to give them an additional hour to deliberate. Two and a half minutes after retiring to the jury room, the members returned with a third not guilty verdict.

Jack Goger still calls the case "the most exciting in which I have ever been involved. Practicing law doesn't get any better than it did in that case."

Later that year, I was honored by the Gate City Bar Association as the first recipient of its Austin Thomas Walden Award recognizing "exceptional litigation skills in an effort to further freedom, justice and equality."

More important than any award, we kept Arthur Langford, Jr., out of prison. He later served as a state senator and continued working for the community until his untimely death. A heart attack took him much too soon. He was only forty-four, but in the second half of his short life he did more for poor people in Atlanta than almost anybody I can think of. Still, if a federal prosecutor and the FBI had had their way, Arthur would have spent the last fifteen years of his life in prison. I'm sorry he is no longer with us. I think of him often, and am reminded of his many contributions to the city.

My law practice continued to thrive, and in 1981, I had the honor of being named by *Atlanta Magazine* as one of the city's top twenty-five lawyers. Even more important to me was the support and respect of criminal defense colleagues like Ed Garland, Bobby Lee Cook, and Al Horn.

Through the 1980s, I began to move away from criminal defense law. Quite honestly, I was shaken by some of the heinous acts committed by men who then wanted me to keep them out of prison. Of course, I believe in the presumption of innocence and the right of every defendant to competent legal counsel, and I loved to stand before a jury and fight for the rights of my clients. But when a man admits to me that he has committed murder, shows absolutely no remorse, and wants me to keep him out of prison, I can't feel good about representing him.

So I decided to create a new kind of law firm, a partnership that would allow African-American attorneys to demonstrate their competence in areas other than criminal defense or domestic relations. Of course, that meant I faced a steep learning curve, but I was ready to invest my time to create a new opportunity.

In the midst of that change, I accepted an opportunity to take on a high-profile case, defending William A. Borders, Jr., a Washington,

DC, lawyer charged with conspiring to bribe US District Judge Alcee Hastings, Florida's first black federal judge.

Hastings was accused of plotting with Borders in 1981 to obtain a payoff from two defendants in his court. An FBI undercover agent posing as one of the defendants contacted Borders and offered him $150,000 in exchange for a reduction of the sentences to probation. Borders was arrested as he left a Virginia motel with the agent and a garment bag containing $125,000.

When Borders asked me to defend him, he insisted that I not question him about the facts in the case.

John Shorter and I worked together on the case and got a change of venue from Miami to Atlanta, where we lost the trial in federal court.

Later, Borders refused to testify in Hastings's trial, and was found in contempt of court. Hastings was acquitted, but then was impeached by the United States Senate and removed from office. During the impeachment proceedings, Borders again refused to testify, risking another contempt charge. I wonder about the constitutionality of Hastings's impeachment proceedings, in light of his acquittal. It appeared to be yet another racially motivated attack on an African-American government official.

But Hastings had the final say, when Florida voters elected him to represent them in Congress.

As our law practice continued to evolve, I was deeply honored in 1989 to create a law partnership with Donald Hollowell, a man who, in many ways, was the reason for my entering the law profession. It makes me sad, even now, to say that my friend, mentor, and former partner, Donald Hollowell, died in 2005. I will never forget him.

Several times during my college days, I slipped into the courtroom on Decatur Street and into Fulton County Superior Court to watch him try civil rights cases. His preparation and cross examination were so thorough, and he had such a commitment to the young people he represented that I made it my goal to affiliate myself with him someday.

One of my fraternity brothers back then, Marvin Anderson, had been arrested during the civil rights movement for trespassing at a Krystal restaurant, and Hollowell represented him. A Krystal employee testified that Marvin Anderson had, indeed, attempted to eat at the restaurant, a crime at that time. Then Hollowell asked a question so basic, many lawyers might have overlooked it.

"Would you identify Marvin Anderson for the court?" he asked.

"That's him right there," the woman said, "at that table."

She was pointing in the general direction of the defense table, but Hollowell asked her to be more specific—to tell the court which man at the defense table had committed the offense of trespassing. She pointed to Horace T. Ward, Hollowell's law partner, and said, "There he is sitting right there."

"Are you absolutely sure?" Hollowell asked.

"I am absolutely sure," she said.

"And nobody else at this table was trespassing on Krystal property."

"Nobody else at that table," she insisted, and the prosecutor shifted uncomfortably in his chair.

Hollowell then made his motion to dismiss the charges, which the judge immediately granted.

Of course, that was just one of many hundreds of unheralded cases he tried in city court—cases that he devoted himself to just as thoroughly as he did when he was setting other legal precedents.

Don Hollowell literally took control of a courtroom, not with arrogance but with confidence and competence. When he openly questioned a judge's ruling against him, he would say, "You mean, your honor, that I can't bring that point before the jury?"

"Mr. Hollowell, don't argue with me," the judge would say.

"No sir, your honor," he would respond without a shred of hostility. "Just perfecting the record."

The year before I graduated from Emory Law School, Donald Hollowell left his private law practice when he was appointed the first regional director of the Equal Employment Opportunity Commission (EEOC) of Atlanta, a federal agency created to enforce fair and equal employment opportunities. Upon his retirement from EEOC, I offered Mr. Hollowell the use of our facilities as a courtesy for his profound contributions to the civil rights movement. I was honored just to have him in our office. He later accepted my suggestion that he be "Of Counsel" to the firm, and Arrington & Hollowell came into being.

I have come to respect Donald Hollowell as a prince of a gentleman—a man devoted to his family and his church and one of the most eloquent men I have ever known.

His commitment to his clients became obvious once again when he championed the cause of Preston King, of Albany, Georgia. King fled the country in 1961 to avoid an eighteen-month sentence for draft evasion. He had refused induction into the army because the white draft board members in Albany wouldn't address him as "Mr.," as they did whites.

Donald Hollowell represented King in 1961, and mobilized people in 2000 to write President Bill Clinton and urge a pardon. On Presidents Day, February 21, 2000, President Clinton signed a clemency document pardoning King of all wrongdoing, and King, who had lived in exile in England, returned home for his brother's funeral

Early in our partnership, few minority law firms were involved in the sophisticated and unique legal issues and transactions that occur in corporate and governmental environments. Because of that limited experience, corporations fell under the erroneous perception that minority firms were deficient in these fields, so they were reluctant to hire them. Minority attorneys carried the burden of dispelling the perception without any opportunity for positive interaction with people who held the perceptions.

The American Bar Association (ABA), responding to an initiative from then-mayor of Detroit Dennis Archer, recognized this problem and initiated the Minority Counsel Demonstration Program, which recruited six corporate participants and twenty-one minority-owned law firms, including Arrington & Hollowell.

The program set three important goals:

• To expand the nature, scope, and magnitude of business opportunities available to minority attorneys;

• To expand professional growth opportunities available to minority attorneys; and

• To make the Demonstration Program a model that could be adopted by local and state bar associations.

To achieve those goals, the program—which was neither a set-aside nor an affirmative action initiative—encouraged corporations and governmental entities to retain minority-owned law firms. In some cases, corporations have retained minority and majority law firms as a team to handle a particular matter, so the minority firms can demonstrate their skills.

Our firm's participation in the Minority Counsel Demonstration Program put us before dozens of corporations, many of them Fortune 500 firms. We have developed long-term professional relationships with several large corporations that would have been difficult for us to approach without the ABA program.

I am proud that our firm was featured in *Black Enterprise* magazine as one of the nation's leading African-American law firms, but I don't think of us as "black lawyers." We are lawyers, and damn good lawyers.

We proved that point when many of the major construction contractors in Georgia were placed under criminal indictment for violation of anti-trust statutes. Most of the companies hired historically white law firms, but the Shepherd Construction Company retained my firm as counsel. As the case unfolded, attorneys for the other companies presented a variety of laborious motions in support of their argument that Fulton County Superior Court Judge Frank Eldridge should dismiss the case. Jack Goger and I took a different approach and attacked the statute on which the charges were based. We said the law was too vague to be enforceable. Eldridge announced from the bench that he had been waiting for someone to raise that point and dismissed the indictment. It was a fleeting legal triumph because the state supreme court later overturned the ruling. However, it helped send a signal to other potential white business clients that our firm could hold its own with the "big boys."

As I consider the African-American lawyers in Atlanta who broke down many of the barriers that otherwise would have prohibited me from practicing law, I can only hope that those who come behind me will find that I, in some small way, have helped them enter this noble profession. Like Don Hollowell, Leroy Johnson, and others, I encourage African-American high school students to establish their careers in the field of law. Despite significant advances, we still have too few African-American attorneys in Georgia.

Our law firm has long sponsored a mentorship program that identifies pre-law students at the college level and assigns them to an attorney at the firm. As an additional incentive, the partnership has awarded stipends to recognize academic achievement and provide each student with a book allowance.

Chapter 7

Serving the Community

For twenty-eight years, the people of Atlanta allowed me to work for them in an official capacity, and I still take every opportunity to do all I can for my hometown and my fellow citizens. Until the day my political career began, I had never seriously considered running for office, although my experience working with the Office of Economic Opportunity had left me hungry for more opportunities to help others. Then, Lonnie King, a leader of the student movement, called me one day in 1969 and suggested that I run for the Atlanta Board of Aldermen. Atlanta was about to experience drastic changes. Everybody knew it, and I wanted to be a part of it.

The previous year, of course, had been tumultuous. The assassination of Martin Luther King, Jr., had triggered rioting in more than a hundred cities and sparked protests on campuses all over the United States. Violent confrontations between protesters and police overshadowed the events of the national political conventions that year. There had been no major upheavals in Atlanta since 1966, but 1969 was shaping up to be a historic political year. Ivan Allen, Jr., was nearing the end of his second term as mayor of Atlanta, and by law he could not succeed himself. The white establishment had anointed Rodney Cook as its candidate. Atlanta's local elections were traditionally non-partisan, so it didn't bother business leaders that Cook was a staunch Republican. Many of them supported the GOP in national elections, anyway.

But Cook faced more than token opposition. Among the strongest mayoral candidates in the primary was Sam Massell, a former alderman and the city's vice mayor. Massell was a progressive from a respected Atlanta family that had done well in business and was generous in its support of civic projects. He was also Jewish, and his candidacy represented a major break with tradition.

The race for vice mayor also attracted attention. Milton Farris, a veteran member of the board of aldermen, was a strong candidate. However, he was challenged by a young, black attorney named Maynard H. Jackson. Maynard was young, but not a political unknown. In 1968, this polished, middle-class Atlantan had done the politically unthinkable by campaigning for the seat of United States Senator Herman Talmadge. It was, of course, an impossible quest, but in something of a foreshadowing, Maynard had outpolled Talmadge in Atlanta by six thousand votes. Talmadge was no fool, and soon after the election he hired Curtis Atkinson as an administrative aide to build bridges to the black community.

While these hotly contested races unfolded, another change was brewing. Behind-the-scenes work by Q. V. Williamson, the only black alderman, had contributed to the creation of a new ward seat on the board of aldermen. Elected in 1965, Q. V. had for four years been the lone African American on the city's governing body. He was a fierce warrior for black rights and opportunities, and wanted to see other blacks on board with him. After all, he had for two years, early in his career, worked for the legendary W. E. B. DuBois at Atlanta University. The writings of DuBois, which Q. V. helped type and edit, significantly influenced his own philosophies. Q. V. saw creation of this new ward seat as the means to increase black political power in the city.

The downtown white leadership wasn't ready to give the seat up to a black candidate, so they agreed to back Benny Irvin, a white attorney. The members of the black group, Young Men on the Go, had other ideas. The members had been meeting at Paschal's restaurant and in private homes to come up with a list of possible candidates for the ward seat. Young Men on the Go included, among others, Lonnie King, Charles Black, and Benjamin Brown, who were already veterans of political organizing.

After screening their lists of Ninth Ward candidates, the Young Men on the Go asked me to run.

Through OEO, I had gained a new appreciation of the role that government could play in creating change, and I was more aware of political change elsewhere in the country. I had come to agree with the thesis of George M. Johnson, former dean of Howard School of Law, that attorneys should be social engineers. Beyond that, he argued that black lawyers could be more than advocates for change; they also had the obligation to serve as political leaders because of their legal training. Johnson once said that "far too many of us are still so dependent economically that we are fearful of acting politically independent."

I was ready to act independent politically, and I accepted the draft. The district could not have been more ideal. This new Ninth Ward was located on the west side of Atlanta and included my old neighborhood, all three of the elementary schools I had attended, and the Atlanta University Center. I asked for and received a ruling from the federal government that permitted me to run for office while holding my job at OEO. Then I went to work assembling campaign leadership. Two of the first people I recruited were Lloyd Whitaker, the Emory professor from whom I'd learned much about the art of courtroom procedure, and my friend, Reginald Williams.

Whitaker had to get approval from his law firm to help me. Philip Alston, Jr., one of the senior partners, wasn't keen on the idea. He told Whitaker that he supported Benny Irvin and that he wasn't sure it was time for another black alderman.

Whitaker firmly disagreed, making the case that Atlanta was changing rapidly and its future depended on the sharing of power by whites and blacks. Alston gave his consent and even made out a personal check for one hundred dollars to my campaign. Whitaker became my campaign's finance chairman.

Sarah Craig, who was Charles Weltner's administrative assistant, wrote our slogan: "A New Voice for the New Ninth." I also turned to Weltner's office for other help, asking George Booker for advice. I remembered how much Booker impressed me when he was working on Congressman Weltner's campaign.

My team was inexperienced in many ways, but we were energetic and grateful for advice. Some of our strategies were naïve. The staff tried to attract white voters by leaving my picture off the posters and by playing up my ties to Emory Law School rather than to Clark College.

Although the city was divided into districts and each alderman lived in a different area of Atlanta, we all ran citywide. I agreed with that philosophy, and still do, because it cuts down on racial politics to a great degree. "If Atlanta ever goes to pure district politics," I said back then, "it will tear the city apart." Because when an elected representative is concerned only about the voters in his or her own district, the city as a whole doesn't receive proper attention.

The first people we went to for help were high school and college football teammates along with other friends and neighbors. I remember a small business owner who contributed twenty-five dollars to help pay for a billboard on Bankhead Highway. These were people who couldn't give much, but the fact that they gave at all meant a lot to me.

I was fortunate enough to attract the support of Good Government Atlanta, a progressive, predominantly white group of young business leaders and attorneys. The group included Emmett Bondurant, who would help rewrite the city's charter in the early 1980s, and Michael Trotter, then a young associate at the law firm of Alston, Sibley, Miller, Spann & Shackleford.

I also received help from more established leaders, like Representative Grace Towns Hamilton, who in 1965 became the first African-American woman in the Deep South to be elected to a state legislature. Although our styles differed greatly (she was aptly named, for she was characterized by grace), she saw potential in me.

The campaign gathered steam and we moved into the second floor of 855 Hunter Street where Q. V. Williamson gave us free space above his real estate office. Q. V. was particularly kind to help out since he had some grave doubts about my candidacy. One evening I was going through some campaign materials and I overheard Q. V. and some friends talking on the sidewalk below. "I wanted to give him some help," the veteran politician declared, "but the boy ain't got a chance!"

Luckily Q. V.'s instincts were wrong—for once. My extremely dedicated campaign workers sensed the appeal my candidacy had for young black people all over Atlanta, and they were quick to capitalize on it. While they also tracked down every white vote they could get, the focus was on locking in the support of the black community. The strategy worked well.

Other old friends and football teammates showed up to help. Some volunteers literally came in off the street. A gentleman named Calvin Blackburn, Sr., walked up to me one day, pressed two fifty-dollar bills into my hand and wished me well. A classmate from my fourth and fifth grade years gave me another hundred dollars. Dewey Merritt, who I discovered later was the cousin of the woman I would marry, took on the task of getting 50,000 campaign flyers stuffed into all the public housing mail slots. One of the students from the business law class I taught at Atlanta University spent his evenings and Saturdays personally addressing 20,000 postcards.

It didn't hurt my campaign any that my opponent was not a great public speaker. He frequently bowed out of scheduled presentations or debates, and Clifford Oxford, one of his law partners and a member of his campaign team, would stand in for him. I was able to call attention to Irvin's absence and theorize publicly about whether Oxford would be Irvin's substitute alderman as well.

On October 1, 1969, I was elected by a substantial margin. Massell, with the help of strong support from the black community, became the city's first Jewish mayor. Jackson won the vice-mayor's office with 58 percent of the vote; 96 percent of the black electors cast their ballots for him in a clear signal about who the next mayor of Atlanta might be. Three other black aldermen, Ira Jackson, Joel Stokes, and H. D. Dodson, were also elected.

Q. V. Williamson won his re-election race, and overnight the city had five black elected officials. It was a heady time for us and our constituents. We privately pledged ourselves to an agenda that centered on improving economic conditions for black Atlantans. Every Sunday night, we all met to prepare for the Monday meeting of the board of aldermen and to discuss strategy. We had differences of opinion that sometimes became sharp, especially in later years, but we really were like a brotherhood.

I was the youngest member of the board of aldermen, and I represented the newest political district. My initial committee assignments were not to the influential committees, such as building, purchasing, and traffic, but the lack of prestige did little to dampen my enthusiasm. I was thrilled to be a part of the process, and I worked hard at the tasks that were mine.

I also made a reputation as a somewhat different type of elected official. I'm not a formal person, and I did not hesitate to raise my voice to make a point. This startled my more "dignified" colleagues, but not as much as my insistence that old assumptions and old ways of doing business had to change. I discovered that the aldermen were not in the habit of keeping minutes of their proceedings, and I went about correcting that right away.

Working with my friend Senator Leroy Johnson, I made some noise in another arena, making the best use of my assignment to the lowly Municipal Buildings Committee. In 1970, Muhammad Ali was trying to return to boxing after losing his heavyweight crown for refusing to serve in the military. Ali was at the ebb of his popularity, and his managers couldn't find a public arena in which to schedule a major match.

Fifty-six cities turned down a fight between Ali and Joe Frazier. Then Leroy received a call from Ali's camp asking if he could arrange a fight in Georgia. Leroy had his staff research state law and found that Georgia had no statute governing boxing and no boxing commission. The question of issuing a boxing license was addressed by each municipality.

The only place in Atlanta appropriate for a boxing match of the caliber envisioned was the Municipal Auditorium, the use of which was governed by the Municipal Buildings Committee. Approval from the entire board of aldermen, which might have been difficult politically, was unnecessary, so when Leroy called and asked me, "Can we do it?" I answered, "Definitely." I was only too happy to introduce the appropriate measure and secure its passage. Conservative members of the board were livid, but the municipal code was clear on the subject, and there was nothing they could do about it.

As a member of the Municipal Buildings Committee, I became part of the process at that point, flying to Philadelphia with Leroy to meet with Joe Frazier's manager, Yank Durham. We had to convince Ali and Frazier and their managers that, indeed, we would allow the fight to go on in Atlanta. Durham said he would sign a contract, but only if we could get Ali into a ring in Atlanta prior to the fight.

"We've been down the lane toward a fight with Cassius," the manager said in essence (almost nobody called him Muhammad Ali at the time), "and just before we were ready to go, the arena would be yanked from under us."

We had to prove to the Frazier camp that we could pull it off. So we contacted Hugh Gloster, president of Morehouse College, and asked if we could use the Archer Fieldhouse gym on campus for an exhibition prior to the fight with Frazier. Gloster gave his permission, and Ali flew in for the exhibition, which went off without a hitch except for the broiling late-summer heat in the un-air-conditioned building.

Leroy took the microphone just before Ali entered the ring against a series of three unknown heavyweights, and said, "What we are doing here tonight is making history. We are showing the world that Atlanta is the capital of democracy."

Leroy may have believed what he was saying, and he might have been right, but Atlanta was still far from the capital of goodwill. On the same day that Muhammad Ali re-entered the professional boxing ring in Atlanta, an advertisement in the *Atlanta Journal* read: Nationwide Ku Klux Klan Rally. September 5th, 1970—8 P.M. Stone Mountain, Georgia. Same Place Where Held For 40 Years. Prominent Speakers. Public Invited. Cross Lighting. All Klansmen And Family Invited. Bring Robe. Sponsored By Ku Klux Klan Association Of America.[4]

After the exhibition, Leroy went back to Yank Durham to make arrangements for the Ali-Frazier fight in Atlanta, but Durham reneged on what Leroy had thought was a verbal commitment. Frazier wouldn't fight Ali in Atlanta after all. That's when the promoters turned to Jerry Quarry, the latest "great white hope," and on October 26, 1970, Muhammad Ali returned to the ring, easily defeating his opponent.

While the Ali-Quarry fight made headlines around the world, the day-to-day workings of government were much more important to the citizens of Atlanta. I saw changes that needed to be made that the media would never find interesting enough to cover. Perhaps because of my legal background, I had an appetite for very detailed and tedious work, so I decided to read through the entire municipal code during my first term. Although some parts were amusingly anachronistic (ordinances against livestock grazing in front yards, for example), other sections were riddled with racist language going back

---

[4] *Atlanta Journal*, 2 September 1970, 11-D.

to the days of segregation and even slavery. I set about the work of revising the code.

In another attempt to move away from the status quo, I introduced a resolution urging the aldermen and the mayor to give every possible consideration to women in the search for candidates to fill vacancies on the board. It was the first of many steps I would propose for the inclusion of women in city government. Later, during my years as president of the city council, I would appoint more women to serve as committee chairs than any other council president. For three consecutive years, I appointed women to chair six of the nine committees, including Myrtle Davis as chair of the Finance Committee, replacing Ira Jackson. Myrtle was the first woman to hold that position. Also at my urging, the council appointed Carolyn Long Banks to complete my term on the council.

In an attempt to lessen the opportunity for corruption in city government and to maintain a good reputation, I introduced legislation during my first term on the board of aldermen that prohibited city employees from being employed in positions in which they directly supervised or were directly supervised by an immediate family member, or by a relative who resides in the same household.

I soon learned, however, that no matter what systems one creates to ensure ethical government, unethical people will find a way around them. I also learned that some good and ethical people, when they achieve a certain level of authority, will be accused of unethical behavior. It goes with the territory, as they say, but, even after having grown a thicker skin in my more than thirty years of public life, unwarranted attacks and accusations still hurt.

The pace of change in the Atlanta of the early 1970s was dizzying. Almost everything was in flux. Highway and high-rise construction was revamping the topography of the landscape and the city's silhouette. Men like Thomas Cousins and John Portman were symbolic of the changes taking place. Cousins had established himself as one of Atlanta's most imaginative and successful developers. He and Portman, with a number of signature developments to his name, including the Hyatt Regency Hotel, seemed to be remaking the entire face of the city.

Cousins envisioned a dazzling array of new office buildings, hotels, and other businesses in the west side of Atlanta's downtown. He imagined something very different from the railroad tracks and rundown warehouse district he could see from his office window. The linchpin for Cousins's grand scheme was to be a new sports arena. He purchased the St. Louis Hawks professional basketball team and moved them to Atlanta. Then, while the Hawks were playing their home games in Georgia Tech's Alexander Coliseum and attracting a following, Cousins began cultivating support for the proposed arena.

Cousins wooed Lloyd Whitaker away from Alston, Sibley, Miller, Spann & Shackleford to head up the project. Whitaker's first job was to assemble a large parcel of property between the corners of Marietta Street, Techwood Drive, and Magnolia Street. Mayor Sam Massell quickly opposed the project, saying that his interest lay in helping people, not more bricks and mortar. Whitaker and Charles Davis, the city's finance director at the time, devised a plan to move forward.

The facility would be financed through tax-exempt bonds to be issued by the same Stadium Authority that had been created to construct Atlanta Stadium in Summerhill. The city of Atlanta and Fulton County would guarantee the venture. The debt service would be supported by revenues from a joint venture with the Fidelity Mutual Life Insurance Company and other investors.

Cousins and his team got to work cultivating support and even persuaded Massell. The final step was getting official confirmation for the bond sale from the board of aldermen. Cousins expected no problems there.

But the days of a board that rubber-stamped the proposals of downtown business interests were over. I wanted the Omni project to work, but only if blacks stood to gain a fair share of the benefit from it. When the proposed bond issue came up, a group of us stopped the process cold. I insisted upon a written agreement that would guarantee the use of more black contractors and the hiring of minorities and women by the unions. This, of course, was years before mandated minority participation in public works projects, a time when qualified blacks and women were routinely excluded from the process. Without a commitment to our proposal from the developer, I promised to delay the vote indefinitely.

My action put the developers in a bind since they didn't want to lose the highly favorable interest rate or to delay opening the Omni beyond the beginning of the 1971–1972 NBA season. I was counting on their anxiety.

Sam Massell, former opponent of the project, then decided to get things moving along. He came onto the chamber floor to argue for allowing construction, but according to board rules, a single alderman could block the presence of the mayor in the legislative chamber. I made my opposition clear, and Massell left the room—but not before angrily staring me down.

To resolve the impasse, I began negotiations with Lloyd Whitaker, my friend and former professor. Whitaker came up with a proposal we could agree on and suggested we move ahead.

"Let's shake hands on it," he said.

I had complete trust in my friend, but I also knew how business and politics worked, especially when millions of dollars were involved. So I risked hurting Lloyd's feelings by saying, "We're not going to have a handshake on this one. We'll draw up the papers, then you'll sign it, and I'll sign it, and we'll incorporate our agreement into the contract before we vote on the proposal."

Through our negotiation and agreement, I believe we created the city's first equal protection clause.

Another concession we managed was the hiring of a black person as assistant to the arena manager. At that time, the country had no minority managers of major sports arenas. Reginald Williams, who was hired as assistant to Robert Kent, eventually succeeded Kent as manager. Williams would later earn a law degree and become executive director of the Atlanta-Fulton County Recreation Authority.

The success of the black brotherhood in Atlanta city government was built upon the foundation laid by many who preceded us. Standing upon that foundation, I participated in the framing of the resolution which became Atlanta's first fair housing law, supporting federal prohibitions against housing discrimination. I also pushed for the aggressive enforcement of state and federal laws designed to stabilize transitional neighborhoods and pressed the governor to vigorously enforce anti-blockbusting laws.

These should have been basic rights for all Americans, but they were denied to black Atlantans until our early days on the board of aldermen.

I also helped remove an ordinance that called for the dismissal of any city employee who filed for bankruptcy. When an employee gets into financial difficulty, I reasoned, that's the worst time to fire him. My colleagues and I were also able to make sure that all city jobs were covered by equal employment opportunity laws, and we later established the birthday of Martin Luther King, Jr., as a public holiday in Atlanta.

The board of aldermen was a full-time job. We used old dictation machines, and I spent a lot of time writing, rewriting, and redrafting letters and memos. I believed then, as I do now, that I should respond to every letter or telephone call. When people take the time to sit down and write me letters, they deserve a personal response, whether I agree with their positions or not. A few years ago, I was visiting a senior citizens' high-rise on Peachtree Road, where the Buckhead Business Association used to hold their business meetings, and an elderly white woman told me, "As long as I'm alive, I'll vote for Marvin Arrington."

"Why's that?" I asked.

She said, "One time I told you about the excessive taxes on a little old piece of property I owned. I knew you were busy, and I didn't expect any kind of response, but within thirty days my property had been reassessed and the taxes reduced. The tax man said you had sent him a letter asking him to look into it."

That's the highest compliment any politician can be paid—that he was responsive to his constituents. It's also the most difficult compliment to earn. I was able to devote the kind of time it took early in my career, partly because I had some understanding law partners. They considered it part of their investment in the community to allow me to serve the city.

In 1972, a special charter commission completed an analysis of Atlanta's city government. This commission, chaired by Emmett Bondurant, made a series of sweeping recommendations for change. The resulting legislation, which was approved by the general assembly at the end of its 1973 session, called for the abolition of the board of aldermen and the vice mayor position. To replace the board, the thirty-member commission recommended the creation of a city council with its own president. The city council president would assume the power to appoint committee chairs, a prerogative that had once belonged to the mayor. The council would have eighteen members, twelve of whom would be elected from single member districts. The other six would run city-wide, but would have to live in separate areas of paired districts. One intention of this plan was to bolster the opportunity for black Atlantans to elect black representatives.

However, even a major restructuring of city government took a back seat to the mayor's race in the public's attention. Maynard Jackson, the ambitious vice mayor, had announced his candidacy, and Sam Massell had every intention of serving a second term. The choice was a difficult one. Massell had done nothing to provoke hostility from the black community; he had been a conscientious and progressive mayor. On the other hand, people were excited about the possibility of Atlanta becoming the first southern city with a black mayor. There was no way to ignore the racial overtones of the campaign. Early on, Massell avoided racial politics. But he was either too naïve or did an about-face on the race issue when he spoke before the Hungry Club at the Butler Street YMCA and urged the mostly African-American audience to "think white." I knew as soon as I heard the words leave his mouth the race was over for Sam Massell.

I was living at 361 Ashby Street near the westside neighborhood of my youth when I declared my candidacy for an at-large council seat, representing the new third and fourth council districts. The combined population of these districts was 89 percent black. I won the election as councilman from Post 14, at-large without opposition. I was one of nine black city council members, along with nine white members.

With Maynard Jackson as our newly elected mayor, having taken 59 percent of the votes, I knew my first four years in city government had given me just a taste of the exciting changes to come.

In the midst of the campaign season, I had been drawn into someone else's political battle. Governor Jimmy Carter had appointed David Gambrell to fill Richard Russell's unexpired US Senate term when Russell died. In 1973, Gambrell was running for re-election to the position he held by appointment. Sam Nunn, another attorney, also entered the race. Nunn was not well known, and he sought me out to ask for my support. I agreed to back him, although I'm not sure why I did. Maybe it was because he was an Emory graduate. More likely it was because he tracked me down and asked me.

Soon I received a call from Gambrell. "I thought you supported winners," he said. I didn't have very strong feelings about either candidate, but this attitude didn't sit well with me. I assured Gambrell that I was, indeed, backing the next senator. Nunn won the race and went on to establish himself as one of the nation's most influential legislators.

In the early days of Mayor Jackson's first term, the African-American council members rarely disagreed about rights for black citizens. Securing those rights dominated Jackson's agenda. Critics claimed he tried to force change in a heavy-handed way, but it was hard to argue with his goals. One of his first initiatives was to bring more blacks into city government. This process went forward smoothly, but changing the police department was a different matter.

We tried to establish a working relationship with John Inman, the police chief, but he took offense. He basically said that he didn't need us to tell him how to run the police department. We didn't want to run the police department directly; however, we all wanted to end the long-standing practice of looking the other way when police, usually white, were unnecessarily rough with black suspects and prisoners.

I was chairman of the Public Safety Committee and was happy to jump into the battle. I criticized Inman publicly and he responded by calling me "an irrational individual who goes off half-cocked." In one of my less guarded moments, I stepped beyond the bounds of propriety when I answered, "I may be irrational, but John Inman is one of the dumbest men I've ever met in my life."

In a more civil tone, I later said it was time for John Inman to move on. We needed new leadership. But he fought us tooth and nail. Finally, we got the votes on the city council to fire him, but he refused to leave.

When Maynard Jackson appointed Clinton Chafin to go down and take over as police chief, Inman had his allies armed to prevent Chafin from going into the chief's office. I was there that day, and I thought there was going to be a shootout.

Then Inman took the fight to court—but not Fulton County court, where he would have had a tough time winning. Instead, he took advantage of the portion of the city that spills into DeKalb

County, which was much more conservative on racial matters in those days. He shrewdly filed suit in DeKalb County Superior Court, where he found a judge to issue a restraining order on his termination.

Fulton County Superior Court Judge Jack Etheridge responded to the order by saying it wasn't a DeKalb County issue—that the tiny part of Atlanta in DeKalb County was an insignificant percentage of the total Atlanta population. The issue, he believed, should have been settled in Fulton County courts.

In response, we made our own end run by reorganizing the government to create the position of commissioner of public safety to whom Inman would have to report. Jackson appointed A. Reginald Eaves, a friend from his Morehouse days, to the new job. Eaves quickly set in motion a process to promote black patrolmen to positions of authority within the department.

While this was going on, the mayor also launched an attack against the city's entrenched economic interests. I helped him push through new policies to assure the fullest possible participation of black business people in work done for the city. The white-owned construction firms, vendors, and consultants could no longer assume they would get the contracts they had enjoyed for years. Building on the momentum we created with the Omni contract, city hall was now demanding a piece of the action for blacks, through set-aside programs and joint-venture partnerships.

This outraged the white business community. Atlanta was about to build an enormous new airport, and these leaders argued that Jackson's policies would make it impossible to complete the project on time or on budget. Jackson would prove them wrong when the new airport was finished on time and within budget. However, Atlanta's historic pattern of good will between the business establishment and city government had almost disappeared, replaced by virtual open warfare.

Jackson stood his ground and did not sugarcoat his reforms by promoting peaceful transition. For example, he hired Emma Darnell as head of administrative services and chief liaison to the business community. This decision exacerbated an already difficult situation. It was rubbing salt into the wounds of downtown leaders and city hall department heads to force them to deal with a woman who took no pains to hide her anger and disdain toward them. Jackson would come to regret his decision later when his relationship with Darnell grew so tension-filled that he fired her.

At that time, to be black and in elected office was to invite criticism and scrupulous attention from the press. Reporters took particular delight in searching for activities of black officials that might represent conflicts of interest. I was one of their favorite targets, probably because I tended to voice my criticisms on the record and because I was a criminal defense attorney for defendants some people thought didn't deserve lawyers.

I was on the hot seat during June of 1973 for just such reasons. Early one afternoon, Atlanta police had started to arrest three black Muslims in front of the Woolworth store on Forsyth Street after an altercation between them and a street preacher. The police efforts led to a fight during which one of the Muslims snatched the gun from the holster of one of the officers. He shot one policeman to death and wounded another in the leg.

I didn't know anything about this incident until a Muslim attorney, Edward Jocko, called me from New York. He asked me to defend the young men. I responded that taking this case would be an obvious conflict of interest for me. However, I did agree to let the men know that a lawyer of their faith was in the process of arranging counsel for them.

I went down to the city jail and signed in. To my surprise, one of the men charged was a friend from Clark College, who in those days was known as James "Sticky" Collins. I was not surprised to discover that the dead man's fellow officers had beaten all three defendants mercilessly. I let them know that legal help was on the way and left.

A reporter soon discovered I'd been to the jail and called to ask me some questions. I made it clear that I was not representing these men. I added gratuitously that even if I were, in my opinion it would not be a conflict of interest since they were charged with murder, a state crime. The next day's paper informed readers that Marvin Arrington, city councilman, was defending Muslims who had killed an Atlanta policeman.

As my visibility as an attorney increased, I sometimes took heat for being both a practicing attorney and a part-time public office holder. There is a long tradition of elected officials also practicing law. The city attorney, for example, maintained a private practice in the same suite of offices where he performed his municipal duties. But for whatever reason, the media seemed determined to question the propriety of my wearing both hats.

The dirt digging continued in 1973 when I was a candidate for an at-large seat on the new city council. A local paper suggested that I was violating the city's code of ethics by representing clients in municipal court. I was able to quash that allegation by pointing out that my clients were charged with the violation of state laws and not Atlanta ordinances. I scrupulously avoided serving on the zoning committee to avoid any suggestions of conflicts over liquor licenses and zoning rulings that might involve my clients.

As my practice grew, I represented more people charged with white-collar crime. In 1974, Leroy R. Johnson, my former mentor and the chairman of the Stadium Authority, ran afoul of the law. The IRS had started a field audit of Johnson's tax returns in 1971, alleging that Johnson had understated his income from 1967 through 1970. To make matters worse, when Johnson learned he was under investigation, he allegedly asked local realtor, E. A. Isakson, to sign an affidavit that the unreported money was actually a loan. Isakson reported the request to his attorney, who notified the federal authorities. With Isakson's consent they placed agents in his office to eavesdrop on his next conversation with Johnson. Johnson was indicted on May 7, 1974.

Howard Moore, Jr., Edward T. M. Garland, and I represented Johnson. For two weeks, we argued the case before US District Judge Newell Edenfield. After the government withdrew two of the four separate tax evasion charges, the jury returned a not guilty verdict on the remaining two, but convicted Johnson for obstructing justice. Edenfield sentenced Johnson to the federal penitentiary at Maxwell Air Force Base in Alabama.

Garland and Moore were unsuccessful in appealing Johnson's conviction to the US Fifth Circuit Court of Appeals. Then Johnson learned that Justus Martin, CEO of Robinson-Humphrey and a member of the Stadium Authority, was insisting that we strip Johnson of his chairmanship. Martin said Johnson was a convicted felon, and the rules prohibited him from serving. Martin and other members of the Authority wanted to keep a minority chairman, and they planned to elect me. Johnson came to my house and explained that his career demanded the ability to maintain the status of the Authority chairmanship. He asked me not to accept. This was an extremely difficult situation for me. I explained to Johnson that I was not taking advantage of his predicament, and that whether I took the position or not, he would lose his chairmanship. The Stadium Authority's by-laws included conviction for a crime of moral turpitude as grounds for removal.

I called upon the lesson I had learned from Donald Hollowell, Howard Moore, Jr., Horace Ward, and from Leroy Johnson himself: To be a defender of the system and the Constitution, you give it your best shot. You'll win some and lose some, but when you leave the courthouse, know that you've done your best. Victory is not always measured by wins and losses, as my Howard Law School professor Herbert O. Reid reminded us, and victory does not always mean acquittal. In Leroy's case, we had found a measure of victory. But

Johnson still felt I had betrayed him, and my election to the chairmanship that he had held drove a wedge between us. In the ensuing decades, we have repaired that rift, and I will always remain grateful to Leroy Johnson, my mentor and my guide during my formative years.

As I felt more established in my city council seat, I began to involve myself more in the political future of other black candidates. Specifically, I saw the need for more African-American judges on the local benches. Maynard Jackson shared that goal. In 1976, a judicial vacancy opened up at the Atlanta Municipal Court, and I called a meeting of the city's black elected officials at my house to discuss who might fill it. I proposed that the mayor appoint Clarence Cooper, who had distinguished himself in the Fulton County district attorney's office since his graduation from Emory Law School. Jackson was concerned that Cooper, a quiet and unassuming man, wasn't strong enough for the job. But my long-winded testimonial in support of Clarence helped win my college and law school classmate a seat on the bench as the municipal court's first full-time black appointee. He excelled, of course, and subsequently was elected Fulton County Superior Court judge. He later served on the Georgia Court of Appeals, and in 1994, President Clinton nominated Judge Clarence Cooper to serve on the US District Court, Northern District of Georgia. His nomination was confirmed by the Congressional Judiciary Committee.

Throughout his first term, Maynard made appropriate appointments of qualified African-American candidates throughout city government. In 1977, I supported his re-election bid, a race he won easily. After the election, Maynard asked me to be his floor leader on the council, and I readily agreed. The position was a new one. My job was, in essence, to carry the ball for Maynard on the council floor—to help pass his initiatives. One of my hardest assignments in that regard was dealing with Reginald Eaves, who had overseen the promotion of black police officers to supervisory positions and apparently had exceeded ethical bounds. Reggie was implicated in a departmental scandal that involved cheating on tests for promotion. Growing heat from the public and the press convinced Maynard that he would have to demand Eaves's resignation. The issue came to a boiling point just as Maynard was leaving the country. He didn't have time to arrange a meeting with Eaves, so he asked me to deliver the message.

I invited Eaves and a small group of other black leaders to my house. Among those in attendance were Q. V. Williamson, P. Andrew Patterson, and Andrew Young. The gathering was very uncomfortable. Eaves arrived expecting unqualified support from all present. He was shocked and angry to hear that the mayor wanted him to resign and that we all agreed with Maynard's call for his resignation. We tried to make it clear to Reggie that he was doing great harm to Maynard and the city. An acrimonious discussion went on for hours, until Reggie apparently capitulated.

A short time later, he submitted his resignation, an action he later tried unsuccessfully to rescind. But not before the mayor returned from his trip abroad and appeared on live television to announce Reggie's dismissal—or so we thought. After forty-five minutes in front of the cameras, Maynard never pulled the trigger. It was a strange and embarrassing incident.

As different as we were in style, it was quite an accomplishment that Maynard and I worked together well enough to make numerous changes on behalf of Atlanta citizens. Many council issues were decided by one or two votes. Maynard often turned to me, as his floor leader, to help implement proposed changes in city government. This work tended to bring about scuffles behind the scenes. I sometimes had to butt heads with Q. V. Williamson on the mayor's behalf, and Q. V. was perfectly capable of eating me alive.

"You're a member of the city council, right?" he asked.

"Right," I said.

"You didn't get elected to the executive branch of government, did you?"

His point was well taken. I was elected to serve as a legislator, not as an extension of the mayor's office. I often thought about that, and in later years reminded my fellow council members that their allegiance was to their constituents, not to the mayor. Unfortunately, my admonishments often fell on deaf ears.

At that time, though, Maynard counted on my work as his floor leader to solidify his support. So it came as a shocking disappointment that he did not reciprocate when I asked for his support when I ran for city council president.

In 1979, Carl Ware gave up the presidency of the city council to accept a promotion at Coca-Cola. His departure set off a series of moves by some council members to thwart the succession process. When Carl announced his resignation, James Bond, who was council president pro tem and responsible for accepting the resignation, checked himself into a local hospital. To ensure that his resignation went through in a timely fashion, Carl had his letter hand-delivered to Bond in his hospital room. The person making the delivery then called the clerk of the council from the hospital and confirmed delivery.

Bond, at the council meeting immediately following delivery of the letter, denied having received it, causing the council to delay action on the matter. He was, in effect, making himself council president by default, because without Carl's official resignation he was simply "absent," and the president pro tem stepped into his place. We could not elect a replacement until Carl's letter reappeared for the record.

In the meantime, Bond announced the appointment of new committee chairpersons, setting off an episode that became a messy example of city government at its worst. Once order had been restored, speculation began about Ware's replacement.

Although I explored the possibility of running for the position, the most mentioned name was Michael Lomax, a California native and graduate of Morehouse. Lomax was a sophisticated English professor who had hitched his political wagon to Maynard Jackson's star. Jackson had appointed Lomax to head the city's Cultural Affairs Department and later named him commissioner of Parks and Recreation. Lomax had moved on from there to win election as Fulton County commissioner.

Lomax must have believed the conventional wisdom that said the election was his for the taking. One Sunday morning, he came to my house and let it be known that his visit was a courtesy call. He said I was, of course, welcome to run for city council president, but I had little chance of getting elected. Further, Lomax said he doubted whether anyone, including the mayor, could get the kind of backing he already had in his pocket.

If I had any doubts about entering the race, Lomax's performance erased them. I told Marilyn after he left, "That's it. I'm going to whip his butt."

I reassembled the members of the team from previous campaigns and went to work. Four or five days before the election, when it looked like I had gained the upper hand, I was invited to a meeting at Q. V. Williamson's house. I assumed it was a last-minute opportunity to get out the vote for me. Instead, a group of black city council members told me, "We're willing to endorse you, but here are committee assignments we want when you're elected."

"You guys have got to be joking," I said, and I walked out of the house. If I had let them usurp my authority by letting them make committee assignments, I never would have been effective as council president.

Although I had served as his right arm in the council for four years, I did not want to presume that I had the mayor's support in the race without asking, so I called on him and asked for his endorsement. Maynard refused, saying he wouldn't get involved in a fight between two of his friends. As a consolation prize, he offered to back me within the council.

"I already have those votes," I said. "I don't need your help with them."

I can't remember feeling more "used" than when Maynard turned his back on me. I had fought not only *with* him, but *for* him, sometimes at the expense of my own political goodwill. Now, he wasn't willing to stand up for me.

On primary election day, I easily outpolled all of the other candidates and qualified for a runoff with Lomax. It continued to be "common knowledge" in the white community that Lomax was going to win. Lloyd Whitaker showed me the results of a privately commissioned poll that showed me losing by a margin of two-to-one. I laughed and asked Lloyd how many black people he thought were included in the poll.

I went on to beat Lomax, earning 73 percent of the vote. One newspaper said that calling my victory a landslide was like referring to the Grand Canyon as a hole in the ground. Lomax was gracious in defeat and came by to congratulate me at the victory party and attended my swearing-in.

In my inauguration speech, I said my election was a mandate from the people of Atlanta to give our attention to "the 'underclass'—that shamefully large group of Americans who either are unemployed or, if employed, are receiving wages that allow them merely to survive.

"These people sometimes represent the cream of their community's crop," I continued. "Yet they languish, beyond hope or inspiration, living from day to day, contributing nothing to their communities, and ultimately nothing to the total society. The lines of civic, economic, and cultural concerns that would link them to constructive participation in their communities have long been severed. Such individuals are all around us, and it is to our peril that we refuse to see them."

During my first two years as city council president, which coincided with Maynard's final two years of his second term as mayor, we often overcame personal disagreements and worked together for the betterment of the city of Atlanta. Most of our problems were issues of style rather than substance. We agreed on the vast majority of issues facing the city at that time.

Twenty years later, black leadership in Atlanta still fails this community. We have had three black mayors, and we cannot point to one area that has been totally revitalized. We have had inconsistent success in areas such as Summerhill, Vine City, Mechanicsville, Auburn Avenue, Ashby and Simpson streets, and Dixie Hills. But if you look critically at our black leadership, we have scored no better than a C average.

I do not exclude myself from this criticism, but I can say that I honestly tried to raise those issues, and the mayors did not heed my advice. Former mayor Andrew Young said of me in an interview for this book, "We didn't always agree. But, I usually knew he was concerned about the effects of any policy on poor people."

Not long after my inauguration, tragedy struck fear into the heart of every African-American parent in Atlanta. Black children started disappearing; then dead bodies began to appear. It was the most horrifying time of my life—a time when I had to deal with the issue both publicly and privately. Marvin, Jr., was ten years old, and while I was deeply concerned for all black children in Atlanta, Marilyn and I, for the first time, were forced to consider the possibility that our own son could be taken from us.

Marvin attended the Lovett School for two years coinciding with the disappearances, and every afternoon a bus brought him home and dropped him off a few blocks from our house. Marilyn or I made a point of meeting him every day at that drop-off location so he wouldn't be walking alone, even for just a few blocks.

One afternoon, I was running a few minutes late, but as I drove up Westview Drive, I could see Marvin a few blocks ahead walking up the sidewalk toward home. A car pulled alongside him and slowed to his walking speed. Well, at that point, I hit the gas hard and hit my horn again and again. Marvin turned and looked at me as if I were crazy as I gestured wildly for him to get in the car.

"What are you doing, Dad?" he asked when he had closed the door.

"What's that car doing?" I asked.

"It was just a lady asking if I was okay and whether I should be walking by myself."

Marvin acted like we were all making too big a deal of this thing—letting our fears rule the day. Then came the day they found the body of a young boy in the Chattahoochee River, near the bridge that Marvin's bus crossed every afternoon coming home. From that point on, he said later, every time he crossed that bridge he remembered somebody was out there killing children not much different from himself.

Another afternoon, I picked him up and I had just heard of yet another boy's disappearance. I reminded Marvin of the importance of being careful, not talking to strangers, never getting into a strange car. This time he just looked out the window. Finally, when I finished my fear-inspired lecture, he said, "Dad, please quit talking about that."

So we didn't talk the rest of the way home, and I wondered if it was a good thing to keep a little boy safe by filling him with fear—fear that a ten-year-old should never have to face. I wondered how many other little boys across the city were similarly afraid, and I wanted to stop whatever monster was out there doing this horrible thing to Atlanta families.

As an elected official, I felt helpless and powerless. The mayor was handling the greatest part of the load from a public perspective. He consoled families personally and responded to the media. The crisis consumed his emotional energy, his time, and his staff. Even after fifteen children had been killed, we were fighting this thing on our own. The FBI refused to offer its help until Maynard demanded it through President Carter.

The role I took at this time was to keep the city running smoothly in all other areas. I wanted to take the pressure off of the mayor so that he could handle the heavy public responsibilities. But I could not turn my back completely on the situation. Whenever I had the opportunity, I encouraged parents to watch their children carefully. Responsible adults, it seemed to me, held the greatest power to keep their children out of danger.

I will never understand what motivated Wayne Williams (or what motivates anyone) to kill people. But I am not altogether certain that he committed every murder for which he was accused. It is possible, I believe, that somebody else was out there at the same time—somebody who may still be out there.

Maynard Jackson was scheduled to complete his second term in 1981, and Mack Wilbourn convened a group of black businessmen to discuss whom they would back in the next election. They were ready to support me, if I would run. However, during my campaign for city council president, I had repeatedly promised that I would not use the office as a base for a mayoral candidacy. Those who supported me felt I could renege on that pledge. I did not. I wrote a public editorial explaining that Atlanta needed, neither a black mayor nor a white mayor, but a good mayor.

I also had to consider my family's needs. Marvin, Jr., and Michelle would be going to college in a few years, so financial responsibilities were increasing. The wise move appeared to be for me to continue to build my law practice and take care of my family rather than close up shop to serve as mayor for one or two terms.

Atlanta, at the end of Maynard's second term, faced significant challenges and was about to change almost overnight from a provincial southern town to a major international city. I'm not sure any of us understood what would be required of us. Until the mid-1970s, almost every CEO in town and every managing partner of a law firm had been born and raised in Atlanta. Suddenly new leadership was coming in. A recession-linked crisis at C&S Bank led to the hiring of Bennett Brown, and when Paul Austin stepped down as president of Coca-Cola, Roberto Goizuetta stepped up. Both were newcomers, as were several others being moved into key business and civic positions. At the same time, management at the newspapers was in transition. By the early 1980s, everybody in town was nervous about the change.

Times were frightening for many Atlantans. The media had dubbed us the murder capital of the world. The missing and murdered children crisis hung heavily over the city. Maynard neared the end of his second term and many in the white community feared a second black at the helm would lead to a downward spiral similar to the experiences of Newark, New Jersey; Cleveland, Ohio; and Gary, Indiana.

Many black business leaders, and Maynard Jackson, believed these changes were—either a part of, or certainly might contribute to—a growing polarization of the city along racial lines. Maynard had insisted on affirmative action in construction of the new airport, and that made many in the white community angry. They saw affirmative action coming to an end if they had a mayor who didn't believe in it and could help the business community to reject it.

Such a monumental step backward could have devastated the African-American community, just as we were using its political power to foster economic prosperity for all. Affirmative action is good business from any perspective, giving everyone an opportunity to prove his or her value and ability.

Many Atlantans disagreed with that viewpoint, however, and they were willing to spend money to push African Americans out of the mayor's seat. The rumor mill reported that a group within the white community had raised $2 million for Sidney Marcus's campaign. They previously had tried to get Jack Watson, President Jimmy Carter's chief of staff, to run, but he turned them down.

No black candidate could raise that kind of money. The best chance we had against such a war chest was to identify a candidate with an established reputation, who could build a new coalition among all Atlantans and help keep the city moving forward.

Andrew Young, former congressman and former UN ambassador, was the perfect choice. He won the election against Marcus and immediately called upon his experience and his contacts to move Atlanta forward. Andy had served on the Banking Committee in Congress, so he knew where the money was. Who else would have thought to seek investment money from Holland? Andy knew they were oil rich, with companies like Royal Dutch/Shell recycling petrodollars in their holding companies.

The first investment money into Atlanta after Andy's election was Dutch money. They put in the two Ritz-Carlton hotels and Monarch Plaza; they bought Phipps Plaza and Perimeter Mall. That was a $2 billion infusion of capital. Not another mayor in America had the combination of banking background and international experience of Andrew Young.

In his personal dealings, Andy started with the assumption that he got along with everybody. We didn't always agree on issues. We sometimes vehemently disagreed. But I knew he was a rainmaker—someone who could put Atlanta on the map internationally.

The attribute that made Andy a great mayor was his confidence. He didn't worry about me or anybody else trying to steal the limelight from him. He'd been there already. He let Shirley Franklin run the city administratively, while I handled legislative issues. The system ran more smoothly during those eight years than at any other time of my service. And it was a good thing, because the city had money problems when Andy took office. It seemed the city always had money problems, a situation that instinctively made everyone defensive—especially when a new administration moved in. Nobody wanted to be "downsized." At the same time, we had to balance the budget. So Andy froze every position in city government. We didn't fire anybody, but we didn't hire anybody, either. Then we moved money around from place to place and kept everything moving.

Andy freely admits that he didn't work well with the city council. He took for granted that everybody in city government was working for the same people and for the same goals. He didn't lobby the city council, and he didn't cut deals with council members. His many absences from the city, even though his travel was vital to our economic success, hurt him on local issues.

"I figured the council would either vote my programs up or down either way," he said.

Many of his proposals were voted down the first time through, and then were approved later.

Although he was criticized for traveling so much, Andy didn't use city money to pay his expenses. Usually, he went with the Atlanta Chamber of Commerce or the Visitors and Conventions Bureau, and they paid his way. He later said he regretted not including city council members more in the marketing of Atlanta worldwide. But even if the money had been there, we had a city to run back home. And all that travel, he insisted, was not as glamorous as it looked.

"There's no magic to going around the world knocking on doors at businesses you know are looking to expand into the United States," he said. "It's simply a matter of good research—of establishing good relationships."

Andy insisted that his success was not the result of his previous international exposure. Rather, his success came from hard work. For example, nobody in Japan knew Governor George Busbee when he first called on that nation in the late 1970s. But he went there regularly and let people there know they were welcome in Georgia. And they came.

Even when he was at home, Andy was selling the benefits of our city to potential investors. He had a policy that I saw work effectively many times. Whenever business people considering a major investment in Atlanta dropped by city hall on a moment's notice and wanted to shake his hand, Andy believed he could always drop what he was doing and spend five minutes with them.

When we remodeled city hall, we had an additional room built near the mayor's office and one near the council chambers. Andy made those rooms pay for themselves many times over. His secretary would invite the potential investor in and serve coffee, while Andy looked for a convenient opportunity to slip away from whatever business he was conducting. Then Andy would meet with the investor for two or three minutes, and they would have their picture taken together. Andy would thank him or her for coming, and in ten minutes, it was over.

One year when the newspapers were making such a fuss about Andy's being out of the city so much, he met 152 business leaders in that office. That's three a week.

But that's not all he did. When he gave visitors his card, Andy wrote his direct phone number to his desk and his home phone number on it. "If you have any trouble," he would say, "you call me directly."

Not too many called, but many of them, particularly investors from Japan, where government carries a lot of clout, felt good about going home carrying a picture with the mayor along with his home phone number. That alone might lead a company to locate in Atlanta instead of some competing city. And the competition was, and still is, fierce.

Andy Young had a greater vision for Atlanta than perhaps any other mayor in our city's history. He saw what we could become, and he took us in that direction. We should always demand that kind of leadership and vision from the mayor's office. Otherwise, we are destined to be caught up in the petty politics of the day.

While he brought in investors, I worked with the city council and Andy's administration to run the city's day-to-day operations, doing some exciting and innovative things. For example, we had an opportunity in the early 1980s to show the best side of city government—the side that gets things done and makes a positive difference in the community.

At that time, our city operated a zoo that was an embarrassment. The lack of care for the animals had become a nationally publicized disgrace. Willie B., the gorilla, swung from a tire on a chain inside a concrete cell while watching television all day. He became a poster child for bad zoos. Our zoo was described years later in a retrospective newspaper article as the "worst zoological ghetto in the nation."

I'm no zoologist, but I was incensed by this glaring shortcoming of our growing city. I called together some of my friends and colleagues to see what could be done. Lloyd Whitaker, A. H. "Billy" Sterne, Horace Sibley, Bob Petty, and I talked at length. We decided to explore the possibility of floating a bond through the Atlanta-Fulton County Recreation Authority (the former Stadium Authority) to underwrite the massive cost of redeveloping the zoo. I was chairman of the authority, and I believed that with strong leadership and community involvement, we could do it.

I tried out the idea on the Recreation Authority's attorneys, who told me it wouldn't work. After I reminded them that they were being paid to find a way to make it work, they found a precedent case in Kentucky. There a community had defined a zoo as a recreational facility, thereby making it eligible to float bonds just like a sports arena. That was the help I needed to maneuver, and I was able to push through enabling legislation for $16 million worth of bonds.

To my critics, I answered that a world-class city deserved a world-class zoo. With a fresh administration directing a new, nonprofit organization called Zoo Atlanta, volunteers launched a fund-raising campaign that eventually generated $7 million from the private sector to supplement the bond revenues. Today, Friends of the Zoo has more than 50,000 members, making it one of the largest support groups of its kind in the nation. The zoo was transformed, and I'm happy to say is now recognized as one of the finest zoos in the country.

We will continue to reap dividends from our investment for years to come with the arrival of two giant pandas, making Zoo Atlanta one of only three places in the United States where visitors can see these beautiful animals. Who could have imagined such a prize in 1984?

My goal as city council president was to achieve similar success in all aspects of government. At the same time, I continued to run my law practice. The job of city council president is part time, at least in theory, and comes with a part-time salary. As I have said, I took care in the clients we accepted to avoid any conflict of interest. Despite that, however, throughout my service as city council president, I faced questions from the media and political opponents regarding a perceived "conflict of interest" within my law practice. The contacts Arrington & Hollowell made with large corporations came not through my political position, but almost exclusively through the American Bar Association's Minority Demonstration Project. We also knocked on doors and attended conferences to meet potential clients. We primarily did employment work and insurance defense work for those large corporations.

It's interesting to me that while people constantly raised conflict-of-interest questions about my law practice while I was council president, nobody ever questioned whether Maynard Jackson, Wyche Fowler, or Sam Massell—all attorneys—might be involved in conflicts of interest when they held the office of vice-mayor.

The most public issue came in 1984 with the Presidential Parkway, which began when Jimmy Carter announced plans to establish his library in Atlanta, east of downtown on land once designated for a freeway to Stone Mountain. Neighborhood groups that had successfully blocked the highway quickly organized to stop construction on a proposed Presidential Parkway that would link the Downtown Connector of the interstate highway system to the Carter Library.

My brother was interested in becoming a subcontractor on the project, if approved, so he and I went to Tom Moreland, director of the Georgia Department of Transportation. I made full disclosure to him, informing him about our plan to get into the trucking/dirt hauling business. I knew that in many instances the city had to pass local legislation in conjunction with state projects, and I wanted to make sure I was operating in accordance with the law. Moreland said our proposal looked fine.

Indeed, an ordinance was needed for the project with approval by the city council. Because of my brother's and my connection to the project, I knew that I would abstain from any vote.

When the issue came to a vote, I hit the yellow "abstain" button, as planned, and nobody said a word. At the close of the council meeting, someone called for reconsideration. I called for a second vote just as council clerk Larry Dingle walked up to me. I spoke with Larry briefly, then turned and hit the green "yes" button by mistake.

I immediately said, "I made a mistake. I meant to hit the yellow button."

But neighborhood people knew about Arrington Enterprises, and they were looking for an angle to break down negotiations on the parkway. My slip-up gave it to them. The mistake I made, which I regret to this day, was in presiding over the debate. I should have turned over the gavel to someone else while other council members discussed the Presidential Parkway.

Attorney General Michael Bowers, who was asked to investigate, later said, "The whole thing was atypical . . . more of an oversight than anything intentional, because I really believe that Marvin tries to play things straight." But the prevailing sentiment at the time among those who wanted a symbol of crooked politicians and a sacrificial lamb was that I fit the bill. Led by opponents of the parkway and fanned by highly critical stories in the media, criticism of my behavior intensified sharply. During the investigation, Tom Moreland never mentioned to anyone that we had met previously and discussed my role in the company. In fact, he later disqualified me as a subcontractor.

Years later, when Moreland went out on his own in private business, he bid on a city contract and stopped by to visit with me and get my support. I reminded him of the irony—that when I needed his support to clear up a matter where I had made full disclosure, he had remained silent. He apologized and said he should have made his position clearer.

Wanting to show support for me in the face of such harsh criticism from anti-parkway activists and the press, several distinguished members of the community decided to honor me at a special dinner in the ballroom of the World Congress Center. The event was organized by the Reverends Cameron Alexander, Cornelius Henderson, Joseph Lowery, and several others. Some 5,000 people attended, including Maynard Jackson, who served as master of ceremonies. I truly appreciated Maynard's stepping up to the podium for me.

Around this time, he asked for my support in the 1987 election, which was nearly two years away. He was preparing to announce his candidacy to return to the mayor's office, and he asked me to endorse him at an upcoming forum of the Hungry Club at the Butler Street YMCA. I told him that I would support his candidacy, when and if he announced, but that an endorsement prior to his announcement would be premature. His probable opponent, assuming I did not run myself, would be Fulton County Commission Chairman Michael Lomax. The irony did not escape me that several years earlier Maynard had refused to endorse me publicly in my race against Lomax, and now he was asking for my public support.

I was not about to endorse a phantom candidate, however. Maynard wanted me to say something like, "I'm encouraging my old friend Maynard to run, and I'll support him."

What I did say was that I found the former mayor's candidacy "extremely attractive."

After Maynard officially announced his intentions, I raised $25,000 for his campaign. Michael Lomax bowed out of the race prior to the election, and Maynard was elected almost by acclimation.

I anticipated a good working relationship with Maynard in his third term, and I believe he did, too. Early on, he came by my house one Sunday morning. He knew I liked to get out and walk for exercise, and he said he wanted to join me on that day. We went up to Mays High School and started around the track.

He asked what ideas I had in mind for the city, and I said I thought some specific things ought to happen. He was all ears.

"We have to do something about the infrastructure of the city," I said. "Our water and sewer, roads, and streets are going to crumble beneath us if we don't address them soon."

He agreed and suggested that I create a committee to make recommendations. I took that ball and ran with it, and throughout 1990, our committee met often and came up with some wide-ranging proposals. We presented our report, and the mayor summarily dismissed it. He said he needed to create his own task force. I was furious, and I told the mayor so. But he disregarded my anger and my committee's work.

When making recommendations regarding the infrastructure, I urged the city council to appoint a legislative liaison between our body and the Georgia General Assembly. Mo Thrash, a lobbyist, came in via contract, and when the mayor found out, he blew his stack. Only one person represents the city at the state Capitol, he said, and the executive branch identifies that person. I responded that the city council is a legislative body, and we need somebody to watch over legislative issues.

City Councilman Tom Cuffie, a strong ally of the mayor, initially characterized the hiring of a city council liaison as one of the brightest things I had ever done. Three or four months later, at the mayor's insistence, he led the charge to overturn our action.

These were not huge issues, just disagreements about the operation of the city. Over time, though, the issues would become more personal. For example, Marilyn and I had a small party at our home to which we invited, among others, the Jacksons, State House Speaker Tom Murphy, Attorney General Mike Bowers, and his wife. Several of my clients also attended. Three or four months later, Maynard accused me of trying to undermine his authority by having state leaders at my house. Of course, if I had wanted to undermine him, he never would have known about the party in the first place.

My style and Maynard's, as anyone who knows both of us will attest, differ greatly. Maynard came from an old-line aristocratic family and was a model of urbane poise with the silver tongue of a preacher's son. He exuded formality, sometimes to the point of being aloof.

I, on the other hand, grew up in a solid, religious, poor family. I had to work hard for everything I have, in an environment that many times was anything but formal. I'm street smart, a little rough around the edges, and I pulled myself into the middle class by years of hard work. While Maynard's legal experience came from the National Labor Relations Board and his private bond practice, I earned my battle scars in the forge of criminal trial practice.

Maynard may have believed he had my best interests at heart when he began to offer me some of the instruction he must have received as a boy from his family, or perhaps he was embarrassed for me that I was so comfortable talking in the language of my neighbors. For whatever reason, he called me to join him at the podium during a meeting. I walked up expecting to discuss the issue at hand. Instead, when I got to the podium he said, "Marvin, you used improper grammar there."

I said, "What?"

"You used improper grammar in that sentence."

I smiled and said, "Mr. Mayor, I graduated from Clark College and Emory Law School, and I understand the rules of grammar as well as anybody. If I decide to break one of them, I do it for effect."

I'm as comfortable with street language as Sam Irvin was with the dialect of the hills of North Carolina. The incident with Maynard was small, but telling. Little differences grew into larger ones, and my friendship with the mayor continued to deteriorate.

I have always been an independent person, and I refused to hold my tongue in public if I disagreed with the mayor. At one particular meeting that Maynard organized, I voiced my opposition to his viewpoint. Afterward, he called me into his office and said, "When I invite you to a meeting, I do not want you to openly disagree with me."

"Mr. Mayor, we have a bicameral government," I answered. "The executive branch of government and the legislative branch of government, and part of the process is for us to debate issues. Under the First Amendment to the Constitution, I have a right to speak up and disagree. You have your viewpoint and I have mine, and we just disagree."

I did not let my disagreements with Maynard affect our success on issues important to the city. Toward the end of the 1980s, for example, I contacted my friend Marshall Hahn, CEO of the Georgia Pacific Corporation, about fixing up eighteen dilapidated homes that had become a neighborhood hazard near Clark Atlanta University. Georgia Pacific donated $1 million from its Project Hope program;

D. Raymond Riddle, president of Wachovia Bank of Georgia, offered construction loans and low-cost home loans; H. J. Russell & Company managed construction; Post Properties provided beautiful landscaping; the city of Atlanta repaired streets and sidewalks; and employees from Georgia-Pacific Corporation donated their time to make many of the renovations.

The result was Faculty Row, on Beckwith Place, a neighborhood of attractive homes for Clark Atlanta University faculty and staff that yields a tremendous benefit to the city.

This is the kind of partnership the city must be willing to make with corporations in an effort to continually improve our standard of living.

While I worked closely with business interests to address the needs of all citizens, I had to chastise the Atlanta Chamber of Commerce loudly for failing to observe the Martin Luther King, Jr., holiday. I had introduced legislation early in my career in city government, only to have it delayed and laid aside. John Lewis reintroduced the legislation later, and it was finally approved by the council, but in 1991 the chamber of commerce in Dr. King's hometown still did not observe the holiday. I considered the situation shameful, and I told them so. They took my criticism to heart and now close their offices in honor of Dr. King's legacy.

Maynard, of course, fully supported these issues. We disagreed strongly, however, over the fate of Atlanta-Fulton County Stadium. As chairman of the Stadium Authority, a post I held for thirteen years, I thought we should turn it into a world-class soccer stadium rather than demolish it. We had built the stadium for $18 million, and when we demolished it, it was valued at approximately $80 million. To replace it now would cost three times the original cost. I told the mayor in a telephone conversation that I didn't see any reason to tear down an $80 million facility. He reminded me that I was just an appointee to the Stadium Authority and that he had given me this base of power.

I said, "Mr. Mayor, I appreciate that fact, but at the same time, I need to maintain a degree of independence and vote for things as I feel appropriate. It's nothing personal. I'm just looking at the merits." He became salty and hung up.

In fact, the new Atlanta stadium cost $1.7 billion (filled with revenues from tickets, television rights, licensing merchandise, and sponsorships). These costs supported my suspicion.

Later, when I returned to Atlanta from a National Bar Association meeting, several friends asked why Maynard had replaced me on the Stadium Authority. I said I didn't know he had done such a thing. Then they directed me to an article in the *Atlanta Journal-Constitution* that announced my replacement. Maynard, I thought, as a professional and a colleague for more than twenty years, owed me the courtesy of a phone call.

He subsequently apologized and said he thought someone from his staff had called me with the news.

The environment turned even more hostile with Bill Campbell and Thomas Cuffie as Maynard's floor leaders. We engaged in some vicious disagreements. When Maynard had to undergo heart bypass surgery, it was reported to me by a reliable source that someone asked him, "Why don't you retire and let Marvin be mayor?"

The response from the man whom I had served as floor leader, carrying the ball for four years, was, "Marvin Arrington will never be mayor by default."

Of course, I had never sought the mayor's office and had made no plans to seek it in the upcoming 1993 election. Several times throughout my career, people asked me why I didn't run for mayor at particular junctures: in 1981 at the end of Maynard Jackson's second term, in 1989 at the end of Andrew Young's second term, and in 1993 at the end of Maynard's third term.

The answer was the same each time. With two children at home facing college and graduate school, I had to put my family and financial obligations first. To serve as mayor, I would have to give up my law practice, and I simply could not afford that.

Then, in 1993, I faced a series of serious charges that were never substantiated, but were so broadly disseminated that I may never outlive the repercussions. Let me offer some background.

City Councilman Ira Jackson introduced me to Harold Echols in 1981. Echols owned airport businesses operating food, beverage, and vending concessions. Over the years, he would call occasionally and want to have coffee or just a few minutes to talk. I gave him some of my time—just as I would any constituent.

The first time I began to suspect problems with Echols was when Councilman Robb Pitts and I were going to an airport conference in Portugal. He walked up to me and said, "I understand you and Robb are going to Portugal. You probably need a little expense money."

He then attempted to hand me a white envelope.

I said, "Harold, I'm not interested."

"No, no, no," he said. "You're my friend, and I just want to make sure you have a good time."

I said, "I'm not interested," and I refused to take the envelope.

I walked into the airport, got onto the train, and rode out to the gate. A few minutes later Robb came up to me at the gate and said, "You won't believe what Harold Echols just tried to do out in the parking lot."

I said, "I know exactly what you're about to say."

Sometime later, when the FBI was questioning Robb on other matters, he told them about the incident.

The other thing Robb told the FBI was that the year that I appointed him chairman of the Transportation Committee, I told him, "The airport looks like it's full of corruption, and some folks are going to wind up in prison if they don't straighten up. You don't want to get yourself in any of it."

Robb reported to me later that he told the FBI about my warning, and that they were surprised by it.

"He told you that?" they asked.

"He told me that," Robb answered. "I remember it verbatim."

Over the years, Harold Echols became a regular at my annual birthday party/fundraiser, usually buying a number of tickets. Every year, we recorded his contributions to the campaign and reported them on the city financial disclosure statement. We also paid federal taxes on the amount that was received.

His contributions obviously had no effect on my work as city council president, because I was trying to cancel the airport concessions contract with the people Echols apparently represented.

Echols requested that I meet him for breakfast at the downtown Radisson Hotel on February 3, 1993. As we finished our discussion, he said he had something to give me. Just as I had on the earlier occasion at the airport, I told him I wasn't interested in any gifts from him. Not only would a gift be illegal, Echols needed the money himself. Everyone knew he was in deep trouble for his illegal activities, and he would need all the money he could come up with to pay his lawyers.

What I didn't know was that he was trying to weasel his way out of a harsh sentence by implicating someone more important than himself—me—in his own legal problems. He convinced the FBI that I was involved in some sort of scheme with him, telling the government that he had paid me to appoint Buddy Fowlkes chairman of the city council Transportation Committee. To prove his point, he attempted give me $500 cash while they secretly recorded us.

His plan backfired because, as before, I refused to take his money. Here is a transcription of the audio version of our encounter, taped by the FBI, as Echols tries to give me the money:

ARRINGTON: No, you can't do that, man.

ECHOLS: Put it in your pocket, man.

ARRINGTON: You don't need to do that.

ECHOLS: I got that other stuff when you want it.

ARRINGTON: What stuff?

ECHOLS: For Marvin, putting Buddy on the transportation.

ARRINGTON: No, no.

ECHOLS: I got it. All you got to do is drop by and let me know when you can.

ARRINGTON: No, no, no, no, no, no, no, no. Harold, you got legal fees. You just keep this money.

ECHOLS: No, put that in. That's spit. You know that. But I made a deal. I can't get that out of Paradies. I didn't even try to get that.

ARRINGTON: No, no, man, don't, don't even, that ain't, that's, forget that. I mean (unintelligible) that wasn't no consideration at all. He deserved that. Forget about that. I would, I would never do that.

ECHOLS: Well, I got it when you're ready.

ARRINGTON: No, no. Don't worry about that.

ECHOLS: All right.

ARRINGTON: Okay.

ECHOLS: Okay?

ARRINGTON: Take care.

ECHOLS: Take care. Bye.[5]

By then Echols was so exasperated by my refusal to take his money, he stuck the $500 into my jacket pocket as I turned and walked away. At that point I had two options: I could take the money out of my pocket and throw it at Echols as he walked away, or I could treat it as a campaign contribution, report it and pay taxes on it just as I would any other cash contribution to my election campaign. I chose the latter course.

---

[5] FBI transcript, 21 December 1993, as recorded by Patti Allen, official court reporter, Northern District of Georgia.

Campaign contributions from Echols were not unusual, although this was his first cash contribution. My records indicate that he or his companies contributed $5,000 over a thirteen-year period. His contributions usually coincided with my fund-raising birthday party early in the year.

Fifteen minutes after Echols put the money in my pocket, I was back in my office ensuring that it was properly recorded. I gave the money to Michael Haynes, one of my accounting clerks, who immediately made a copy of the bills. This was Michael's standard practice with cash legal fees to keep a record for accounting purposes.

My secretary was equally efficient, and within hours, she had typed a letter thanking Echols for his $500 political contribution. At 1:58 P.M. the same day, the cash was deposited in my campaign account at Wachovia Bank.

I also reported the contribution on my political campaign's income tax return as well as to the city of Atlanta, which requires reporting of all contributions.

Two days after my secretary mailed the letter to Echols, he called and insisted that the $500 was not a political contribution, but rather for my personal use. I told him that I don't accept gifts of that kind.

I learned later that Echols had also tried to implicate council member Morris Finley in illegal activity. He called Morris to a hotel parking lot to talk. While they were there, Echols tried to put money in Finley's pocket. Finley hit his hand and said, "Man what are you trying to do?" Then he got in his car and left. The whole thing was taped by the FBI. Echols was busy trying to save himself.

It came as no surprise to me when I learned in October 1993 that Echols had been cooperating with federal authorities by permitting his conversations with me to be taped. What did surprise me was that the federal prosecutor would give credence to this man who admittedly lied to a grand jury more than one hundred times. Echols faced more than 150 years in prison, if convicted of all the charges against him—charges that included extortion, perjury, witness tampering, obstruction of justice, money laundering, income tax evasion, racketeering, and bribery. Yet, he was the one the FBI trusted. In November, despite that stack of charges against him, Echols received only a two-year prison sentence and a large fine.

Anticipating the public release of Echols's charges against me in December, I submitted to a lie detector test, the results of which further exonerated me of any charges.

In 1994, Echols testified that he gave money to Bill Campbell, Ira Jackson, Buddy Fowlkes, and me.

Here is an excerpt from a transcript of a proceeding involving Echols:

JUDGE ANTHONY ALAIMO: Did you pay Mr. Campbell anything?

ECHOLS: I gave Mr. Campbell some money out of that, yes sir.

By that time, though, the damage had already been done to me. The federal prosecutor, Sally Yates, had played the FBI video in open court, even though it had nothing to do with the matter at hand. She, in effect, slandered me in absentia, accusing me of accepting an $11,000 bribe from Echols. But she never had one fact to back up her claim, and she never gave me the opportunity to defend against her reckless claim in court. I had no forum to defend myself. If she believed her claim, she should have indicted me. But I was never charged with any illegal activity, because I never committed any illegal activity.

Ronald Freeman, president of the Gate City Bar Association, along with two other African-American lawyers, deplored the prosecutor's tactic in a letter to the *Atlanta Journal-Constitution*. "The government . . . harmed Arrington in a way that can never be repaired," they wrote.

It was a serious threat to my credibility. Even so I refused to let the Echols matter dampen my excitement as we prepared for the 1996 Olympic Games. The effort, which had begun years earlier, was moving quickly toward its culmination. The games would prove to be three of the most important weeks in Atlanta's history.

It was the event of my lifetime. Seeing our city transformed, meeting some of the greatest athletes in the world, watching Muhammad Ali light the Olympic flame—these are the images etched permanently in our memories. Seeing Ali was particularly moving to me. Twenty-six years earlier I had done the behind-the-scenes political work that allowed him to get back into the boxing ring, and now he was back in Atlanta moving us all to tears.

To the world, that moment was the beginning of the Centennial Olympic Games. To those of us in Atlanta, however, it was the culmination of years of preparation.

Early in that process, when we were telling the world about the merits of our city, I traveled with Andy Young across Africa to meet with several African Olympic committees. My role was two-fold: to show those committee members that the Atlanta committee had the full support of the city, and to offer my hand in friendship.

It saddens me to see that some International Olympic Committee members were open to having their votes influenced by inappropriate gifts and that, apparently, some cities were willing to cross the line of propriety in an effort to secure the Games. I never saw anything like that happen in conjunction with securing the 1996 Games. I knew all of the people on the Atlanta committee to be honorable. I trusted them, in fact, with everything I owned.

Early in the bid process, Atlanta Olympic Committee chairman Billy Payne said it would cost millions to put together a successful bid for the games. Key Atlantans would travel the world spreading the word about our city. We would also bring dozens of International Olympic Committee members from around the world to Atlanta. Architects would design facilities so we could show IOC members our specific plans.

Local businesses provided much of the needed capital for all of that travel and preparation, but Billy Payne called on local individuals as well. He came to my office one day and asked me to sign my personal guarantee on a bank loan that the Atlanta committee would eventually pay back with corporate donations. If those donations hadn't come through, however, I would have been responsible for repaying the money. It probably would have bankrupted me.

"I've got a lot of confidence in you, Billy Payne," I said as I signed the note.

"Believe me," he said, "the rest of the money is forthcoming. You'll be okay."

I laughed and said, "Well, if it doesn't, I'm broke. And you'll have me right behind you looking over your shoulder for the rest of your life."

"That's why I'm going to make sure it works," he said.

We all pulled together in a way that I've never seen in Atlanta to ensure the success of the Olympics. One of the most pleasurable aspects of the Games for me was working with my friend A. D. Frazier.

Years earlier, when he was an executive at Citizens & Southern Bank, A. D. Frazier had played a pivotal role in my election to the presidency of the Atlanta City Council. A year later the First National Bank of Chicago called, and A. D. went north. I almost had tears in my eyes the day he left, although I knew his success there was guaranteed.

I was in Chicago on business in the late 1980s, and I decided to drop by unannounced to see A. D., who by then was responsible for his bank's entire North American portfolio of $10 billion in loans. The lady outside his office said, "I don't know if Mr. Frazier will see you."

But when she announced me, he stepped out of his office and we hugged. The executive suite of the First National Bank of Chicago came to a halt as people said, "Who in the world is this black man, and where did he come from?"

Even when he was in Chicago, A. D. had a vision for Atlanta. We were talking about the city and its economic growth, and he said, "One day that corridor that runs from the Omni Hotel to Coca-Cola is going to be an economic highlight in the city of Atlanta."

I knew the potential was there, and that "one day" A. D.'s vision would become reality. When I was growing up, the area just west of downtown was one of the economic driving forces in the city. When A. D. made his prediction, the Coca-Cola headquarters was two blocks away, the Omni stood at the other end, and the Atlanta University center was just two miles away, but everything else was just "potential." Only with proper planning and support from the entire community could it thrive again.

I received a telephone call one morning in 1991, a call that would lead eventually to the rebuilding of that community. Billy Payne called and said a headhunting outfit had identified A. D. Frazier as a potential number two man for the Olympics organizing committee. "Do you know anything about him?" he asked me.

I said, "Billy Payne, everybody talks about your getting to work at 5:30 in the morning. If you hire A. D. Frazier, when you get to the office the coffee and the sweet cakes will be ready. He doesn't know when to quit."

So A. D. Frazier came back to Atlanta and took over the day to-day operations of the Olympics, and he was hugely responsible for the Games's success. Perhaps even more important than the three-week event of the Games, however, was the implementation of the vision A. D. Frazier had seen years earlier, fulfilled with the creation of Centennial Olympic Park and the economic prosperity that surrounds it.

Of course, many people viewed the Olympics only from the perspective of what it could do for them personally. The B. G. Swing deal comes immediately to mind. It, and the tragic bombing in Centennial Olympic Park that left a woman dead and dozens injured, became the worst legacies of the Games—ones that are hard to forget.

Fortunately, after several years on the run, the culprit in the bombing, Eric Robert Rudolph, was finally captured and pleaded guilty to that horrific crime and two other violent bombings, and is serving time in federal prison.

The black eye the city suffered as a result of the B. G. Swing deal still makes me flinch, even today. Oddly enough, when it was initially proposed, the deal looked like a good business opportunity. B. G. Swing was to contract and negotiate with subcontractors for various locations on the streets of Atlanta where vendors could sell their goods.

When we started looking into it, it quickly became clear that the deal had been created through manipulation. Munson Steed, owner of B. G. Swing and a close friend of Mayor Bill Campbell, had hired people to conduct a study to show the potential economic impact at a time when the city was being criticized for not making the most of a fantastic economic opportunity in the Olympics.

When it became apparent that the results of the B. G. Swing study had been exaggerated, it was too late. Campbell already had the votes to approve the deal. I was totally against it at that point, and some of the mayor's people tried to stop it. Some even resigned their positions with the Atlanta Economic Development Corporation to stick by their principles. But the deal went through, and it still haunts the city.

Dozens of vendors lost thousands of dollars because of unrealistic goals and projections. Atlanta police had closed off many of the streets where vendors were located, and some vendors were in locations with absolutely no foot traffic. As a result, vendors, expecting to reap thousands on their investments, defaulted on loans. Some lost their homes. The little bit of money Atlanta made on the scheme, $2.9 million, was threatened by $25 million in lawsuits from vendors who felt they had been duped by the mayor's deal with

Munson Steed, who was indemnified against any losses through his contract with the city.

Beyond those lingering black marks, however, the Olympics allowed us to see the world through new eyes, and for international visitors to know Atlantans personally. We sat in the stands beside people from all over the world. We hosted Olympic guests in our homes. We will always treasure those memories.

The long-term effects of the Olympics are obvious in our city. The event galvanized economic components to move Atlanta forward. For instance, Centennial Olympic Park has blossomed as an economic generator, with condominiums, hotels, and other projects going up nearby. Out of the Olympic movement came the state-of-the-art Centennial Place Elementary School, an exceptional facility created from a unique partnership of Georgia Tech, Georgia State University, and Coca-Cola. When we look at the developments in the Atlanta University Center, Summerhill, and other areas that benefited from the Olympics, we see the lasting legacy of the Games.

The Olympics also gave the city the political cover it needed to move on a proposal I brought forth years earlier. I had proposed that we tear down Techwood Homes. Techwood homes was the nation's first housing project, dedicated by President Franklin D. Roosevelt with hope for raising the quality of life for those who lived there. It became a place where generations of families lived with little chance of upward mobility. I hoped to rebuild Techwood Homes and make special compensation for the residents by setting up a $1 million scholarship fund for the students who lived there. This idea was met with hostile rejection by black community leaders, particularly those living in Techwood Homes. They feared that families would be left adrift with nowhere to go and with few life skills to make it without the support of public housing. Leaders also feared the loss of voting strength that a concentrated African-American community could offer. Even though Techwood Homes was a bastion of poverty and drugs, many felt secure in the neighborhood in which they had grown up. However, the Olympic movement did exactly what I proposed and there was no outcry. Walt Bellamy, a former Atlanta Hawks basketball player, said to me one day, "the Olympic movement is being credited for your idea, and I guess it was well received because it was put forth by the Olympic movement."

We have properly honored Billy Payne, the first man with the vision for the Olympics in Atlanta, by erecting a statue of him in Centennial Olympic Park. We should also place a statue of Andy Young in the park, for without Andy's skills as a former ambassador and his worldwide respect, we never would have landed the Games.

Although the 1996 Olympic Games made a greater impact on Atlanta than any other single event, it is the day-to-day, behind-the-scenes work that has transformed our city over the nearly three decades of my public service.

Chapter 8

The Casualties of War

A Statesman is a politician who places himself at the service of the nation. A politician is a statesman who places the nation at his service. —French president George Pompidous (1911–1974)

As the 1997 campaign season approached, Marvin, Jr., was finishing law school at Emory and Michelle was a sophomore at Howard University. I did not, however, make any plans to challenge Bill Campbell for mayor. Then a series of events brought me into the race.

First, I proposed a Parking Authority for the city, which would generate between $30 and $50 million within five years. This money could, among other things, pay employee salaries and revitalize some of our disadvantaged neighborhoods. Campbell initially said he favored the idea, then he killed it for no apparent reason. Our city center would die if we didn't address parking and transportation needs, and Campbell refused to even consider a solution that would create new revenue at the same time.

Then, one Sunday morning, I saw how petty Campbell could be. I was sitting in church with city councilmen Robb Pitts and Vernon McCarthy when the mayor was speaking. The mayor rose and introduced McCarthy, who was his friend, and went on about what a great job Vernon was doing. Campbell went on with his talk, without any mention of Pitts or me, which was a sharp breach of standard protocol.

Behind us sat Curtis Atkinson, a special assistant to Senator Max Cleland. Curtis leaned forward and said surely Campbell couldn't be that small. We chuckled at first, that the mayor could be so insecure that he would not even introduce his potential rivals in church on Sunday morning. Later, though, I was embarrassed to think that he was the mayor of my hometown. When Campbell sat down, Quincy Carswell—who had invited the mayor to speak—stood and sort of cleaned up the uncomfortable situation by recognizing Robb and me.

Next, it appeared that Campbell and his supporters on the city council were going to get rid of Reggie Williams, who had served well for nine years as executive director of the Atlanta-Fulton County Recreation Authority. It didn't take them long. Reggie had recently lost his wife, who died suddenly at her job at Grady High School one morning, and he wasn't up for a prolonged political fight. I had never seen anybody go after people personally the way Bill Campbell and his administration did. He was ruthless. Worse than that, I didn't see the city moving forward. I decided my hometown deserved a better mayor. So I ran for the position myself and became a witness to the truth contained in the Gospel of Matthew: "For what does a man profit if he should gain the whole world and lose his soul; what shall a man give in exchange for his soul?" (16:26).

They say politics is a dirty game, but sometimes it's an evil game, and when you twist facts the way Campbell did with the tape Sally Yates had used in court earlier, it's just plain evil. Of course, I'm talking about the grainy, black and white tape of Harold Echols and me at the downtown Radisson Hotel, as Harold followed the prompting of the FBI. Nothing has hurt me, politically, more than the Campbell campaign's manipulation of those images. However, when viewed while listening to the accompanying audio, the tapes completely exonerate me. Campbell's people muted the audio portion, then mailed 10,000 copies to Atlanta voters.

The tape, of course, never mentioned that Bill Campbell had been smeared with the same allegation by the same man. Echols said he bribed Campbell when he was a city councilman. The tape never mentioned that Campbell faced vote fraud charges earlier in his career.

It is important to note that former United States Attorney Joe Whitley, who had been prosecutor Sally Yates's boss, said he believed me and endorsed my candidacy. Likewise, former United States attorney general Griffin Bell endorsed me. Judge Bell even went before the editorial board of the *Atlanta Journal-Constitution* and, according to reports, said that anyone who had endured the scrutiny that I had endured without an indictment was "as clean as a hound's tooth." But those endorsements were overwhelmed by the manipulation of the Campbell re-election campaign.

Then the campaign turned even uglier. When the votes were counted and Campbell and I were declared to be in a runoff, Maynard Jackson, who had been a mentor to Campbell, went on television and said that a vote for me for mayor would "set the clock back" on civil rights progress in Atlanta. The comment enraged me. This went way beyond politics. Maynard was impugning my name publicly in the worst possible way.

Maynard Jackson had no idea what I had done for the civil rights movement. He was not even in Atlanta when I marched behind Julian Bond, Lonnie King, and others through our city's streets. He was not here at the height of the movement when we, the college students, forced city restaurants to integrate.

Perhaps he did not remember that I was one of the two men who integrated Emory Law School. And maybe he forgot that I was primarily responsible for integrating the Atlanta Water Works, or that I worked to get Muhammad Ali back into the boxing ring in Atlanta, or that I raised the money for the statue of Hank Aaron at the stadium.

But he could not have forgotten how, as mayor, he later built on the foundation we had laid and, with my help and the help of other African-American city councilmen, we led Atlanta into a new era of race relations. I stood with him through those years, as his floor leader in the city council, building coalitions to ensure that the African-American agenda succeeded.

In subsequent years, we differed, sometimes publicly, on matters of policy, but our relationship took a decidedly nasty turn when Maynard went on television that night in November 1997. Continuing with his vicious racial attack, he called white people who supported my campaign "Lester Maddox types." Maddox is the former Georgia governor, who, as a restaurant owner before his political career, once barred black people from entering his restaurant.

Several days later, while I waited for an elevator following a debate with Campbell, several of his supporters continued the race baiting Maynard had started, even using the offensive terms "sellout" and "handkerchief-headed Negro" as television cameras rolled. The overall effect of this tawdry strategy was to play into what I believe is one of the real shortcomings of Atlanta society: There are serious class divisions in the city, particularly in the African-American community, where class and status are often associated with skin color. It harkens back to slavery, perhaps beyond even that.

During slavery, there was often tension between the lighter-skinned slaves, who usually got to work closest to the slaves' master in the big house, and their darker-skinned brothers and sisters, who were normally relegated to the fields. The darker slaves believed that the lighter slaves considered themselves superior to their blacker counterparts, and the fairer-skinned on the plantation lent credence to this belief through their treatment of the field hands.

That behavior carried over long after slavery was abolished. By linking me to such dreaded stereotypes as the "handkerchief-headed Negro" (think Aunt Jemima) and "Uncle Tom," who were usually portrayed as dark-skinned and considered unsophisticated toadies of the white slave master, my opponents played on those old feelings of superiority among the city's elite and lighter-complexioned African-

American residents and their distrust, even disdain, for their darker-skinned brethren.

Campbell's supporters, unfortunately including Maynard Jackson, knew the right code words to keep some one like me in my place. And they knew how to use those words effectively. If most in the black community would be honest about it, they would admit this sad state of affairs. But it is not a subject that will draw many participants in a public forum. The situation is unfortunate, a kind of deep-seated self-hatred. And I don't know how—or if—we'll ever overcome it. We haven't managed to conquer it 150 years after slavery.

Sometime after the election, a man I'd known for years, who was highly respected in the community, came up to me at a civic function. He leaned over said to me: "The only reason you're not mayor of Atlanta is your skin color."

During the mayoral election, I made the mistake of letting the scurrilous attacks get to me. At one of the debates late in the campaign, I played right into my opponents' hands. My anger got the best of me and I used a slur to refer to Maynard's absence from the city during the days of the civil rights movement. I immediately regretted the statement, and soon apologized for it. But the damage was done. Maynard was an icon in the black community and attacking him publicly was a "no-no." I do not mean that as any kind of slight against him. Maynard was a courageous man, whose history-making election as mayor bolstered the pride and sense of worth of black people across this city. He did much to earn his status as an icon. And, following his sudden death after a heart attack in Washington, DC, in 2003, that status continues to grow.

But, back to the 1997 election. Bill Campbell and I disagreed on several important issues, and yet all people remember of the 1997 campaign was the nastiness—Campbell's personal attacks against me and my personal responses to those attacks. A candidate should be strong enough to withstand the attacks and say in every instance, "I am not going to be a part of a dirty campaign and dirty tactics"—then stay above the fray.

Lee Brown, a former public safety commissioner in Atlanta, won with that kind of campaign for mayor in Houston. If Atlanta voters demand it, we can have those kinds of campaigns here as well.

Chapter 9

Family Matters

I am wounded,
but I am not slain.
I shall lie down and bleed awhile,
then I shall rise and fight again.
—John Dryden

In the months shortly after I left office, having lost that bitter election for mayor, I became very introspective. I knew I was wounded, angry, and licking my wounds, but my life had shown me repeatedly that I would, indeed, rise again. There is just too much that needs doing in this world for me to simply lie down, call it quits, and not get up.

My absence from political life has been a time of reflection for me, considering the accomplishments of twenty-eight years in public office, and honing my vision for the future of Atlanta. In the weeks, months, and years immediately following that loss, Marilyn and I enjoyed quiet time together without the demands of city politics. I came to appreciate even more the sacrifices she had made over the years for our family and for my political career. I tell people that I will forever be indebted to her because she raised two fine children. When I was taking care of the city's business or my own law practice, she made sure they got baths every night, that they did their homework, and that they went out that door every morning with a hot breakfast. And I don't care what anybody says, those are not small things.

We both went to PTA meetings because I wanted to hear, directly from the teachers, how Marvin and Michelle were doing. I took Marvin to little league football practice. But Marilyn was the one most involved in our children's education. She got them to band practice, scouting, soccer, just about everything they were involved in.

As the months continued to roll by, I began to notice a difference about my life with Marilyn. If was as if we were not clicking in the same ways that we had always clicked. Little things each of us did seemed to annoy the other more and more. There were more disagreements about things—how things should be done, what things should be done.

I wondered why I had not noticed this before. Perhaps, because I had been putting so much of my focus on things outside our home—my law practice, city government—that these kinds of things slipped past me. Maybe it was a case of my having deferred so much to Marilyn on domestic and other matters for years because of my busy schedule—and now that I had more time, I was getting involved in things that she was used to handling on her own. Such things can be tricky adjustments that you don't think about until they become problems. But, in any case, something was happening to our marriage. After all of those years, when we both wished I had more time for us to spend at home, it was finally a reality. Yet, it wasn't making us—certainly not me—as satisfied with our situation as I'd always thought I would be.

As time went by, my dissatisfaction grew, and I could tell it was putting a strain on Marilyn. Our relationship became chillier and chillier. Finally, I asked for a divorce. I moved out. The children were understandably upset, and it took a long while for them to accept that things had changed between their mother and me. In 2003, Marilyn and I were divorced after more than thirty years of marriage. And two years later, we're all still dealing with the reality of that change in our family.

Even today, as I look back at the life we had, I am thankful for the quality time I spent with my family while Marvin and Michelle were growing up, but I'm sorry I did not increase that by 25 or 30 percent. Once those days are gone, they're gone. We can never relive them.

What that makes me realize, however, is that what I can do, and the most important thing we can all do to change Atlanta for the good, is to focus on our young people. They are our greatest legacy. I was particularly honored when Emory University presented me with its Emory Medal. In its presentation, the University said, in part:

"Your volunteer efforts reflect your concern for the welfare of all our citizens, but especially for our youth on whose behalf you have fought vigorously to reduce crime and prevent drug and alcohol abuse."

The school also hung a life-size photograph of me on campus alongside great Atlanta leaders, such as Hamilton Holmes, Ben Shapiro, and Robert Strickland.

I was walking across the Emory campus to a board of trustees meeting one day when a young African-American woman stopped me and introduced herself.

"Mr. Arrington, I'm at Emory because of your influence," she said, and her words brought tears to my eyes. That's what it's all about—encouraging others to succeed.

Chapter 10

Back to the Fire This Time

The job of encouraging, demanding, and helping our young people succeed is a serious challenge. That fact is brought home to me every day as I sit behind that bench in judgment of others. I think often about the awesome power of being a judge, and the sometimes disappointingly real limitations. As judge, one watches the worst human dramas take place; watches man's inhumanity to man; watches desperation, violence, meanness, and, often, incredible vileness—and then passes judgment on the guilty parties. The judge is there to make sure the defendants', the victims', and the public's rights are protected. The judge's interest and duty is to see that real, legal justice is served—a big job, indeed.

But, most of the time, when a case gets to you, it is already too late for you to intervene to stop or alter actions that have already changed the lives of everyone in that courtroom connected to that case. Sure, we judges have to believe that our decisions, our wisdom, our thoughtfulness make a difference; that we do, in some measure, help protect society and help make the streets of our communities safer places to be, but most of time, we are on the back end of crime. The damage, for the most part, has already been done. The fear a crime has caused is already hanging over a neighborhood or community and changing the way people go about their daily lives.

We dispense punishment, trying to balance the needs of the victims, community, and perpetrators, trying to arrive at that most difficult outcome we call "justice."

In our hands is the power to dismiss a case, challenge the facts of a case, give a defendant probation, serious jail time, or even the death penalty. The responsibility is daunting, because it is difficult to satisfy all the stakeholders whose interests you must consider. Justice, it has often been said, is in the eye of the beholder. Not only that, but there's a difference between justice and satisfaction. What I have found is that, when most people say they want justice, what they really want is satisfaction, which includes at least some measure of revenge.

Almost any decision you make as a judge is going to tick somebody off. That is why you have to keep focused on the real issues in a case and make your decision based on what you know is right.

That brings me back to the incident that opens this book. The young man accused of being the courthouse shooter, who allegedly killed four people during a frightening, deadly rampage, certainly shook us all up, but that incident was not the first time I've feared my life was in danger because of my service as a judge.

I had a case not long ago involving three young defendants: a white female, a white male, and an American Indian male. The crime took place in the Little Five Points section of Atlanta. These three attacked two young black men on the street for no apparent reason. The black men happened to be brothers. Somehow, the five got into a shouting match and the brothers were beaten, kicked, and stomped.

Many in the black community were outraged. The case was all over the news every night. Two or three years before this incident, the state legislature had passed Georgia's first hate-crimes law, which allowed stiffer sentences in cases that prosecutors successfully argued were motivated by racial or ethnic hatred.

The black district attorney in this case was under pressure from the community to throw the book at these defendants, so he tried the case under the hate-crimes law. I drew the case. I was aware of all of the publicity surrounding the case, but I was determined to judge it on its merits and not let political considerations sweep me away. When the convictions were rendered, all attention was on me. How much time would I give them? Surely, I would throw them under the jail. The expectations were unavoidable. I took my time, studied the case, looked at the law and the lives of the five young people.

I concluded that what took place was an aggravated assault. I looked at the average sentence in my county for aggravated assault. It was 4.8 years. The defendants were young and, I believe, salvageable. The young white female was a vagabond, moving from home to home, and she wrote me a very long letter in which she admitted what she did was wrong and that she was, basically, not that type of person. She said she knew I had the power to lock her up and throw away the key, but she was sorry for what she did, and she wanted a chance to improve her life.

I gave the white male and female sentences of eight years. I sentenced the American Indian male to four years and lectured him severely. I couldn't understand how he—a member of a minority group that suffers much discrimination—could be involved in something like that. I also told the defendants' lawyers that I would make it possible for them to try for an expedited appeal of the hate-crimes conviction, because—in my mind—there were questions about the way the law was written.

The young woman thanked me. The white male said I had gotten his attention, and, likely, saved his life. I believed I had done the right thing.

Many in the community disagreed. Man, did they disagree. Some in the civil rights community and other social activists were incensed by my ruling. They questioned not only my blackness, but my manhood and intelligence as well. A state legislator with ties to the hate-crimes bill and an Atlanta city councilman basically accused me of being a traitor to my race. The legislator threatened to take me before the Judicial Qualifications Council. There were angry letters and phone calls.

But that wasn't the end of it. I was in the grocery store one day, trying to get a little shopping done and get home, when a man ran up to me shouting and threatening me. "You're that damn brother who let them crackers off!" he said. He lunged toward me, but somebody pulled him away. He was still shouting nasty things about me.

Sometime later, The Georgia Supreme Court overturned the hate-crimes statute on grounds that it was "unconstitutionally vague." Before that decision, while I was still in the hot seat, former Atlanta mayor and United Nations ambassador, Andrew Young, had been one of the few community leaders who said I did the right thing in that case. I thought about his kind words when I heard the court's ruling.

Another example of justice being in the eye of the beholder was a case that came before me involving a father who was discovered to have been having sex with his two daughters for years. The older girl was in her second year of college and the younger still in high school by the time this came to court. The father and his attorney decided it would be in the man's best interest for him to plead guilty and ask mercy from the court. I was prepared to give him a very long sentence because I couldn't understand his actions. I have a daughter myself, and it would be repulsive to me to even imagine having thoughts like that about your own child, but this man's daughters asked to be heard before sentencing. They said, in essence, "Judge, we know that he was wrong, but we love our father, very, very much. He is a good man, has always taken care of his family. We just want to start the healing process, start going back to church. You want us to go to counseling, well, we want to go with him, all of us together. We don't want to stop being a family."

The wife spoke up for him, too. She didn't want him to be incarcerated at all. No jail time. I was stunned. I probably gave him one of the lightest jail sentences I've ever handed down. I gave him five years to be served on weekends. Remember, this was a child molester.

But once he got the sentence, and everybody agreed it was a great sentence (for him) under the circumstances, he started filing all types of appeals: lack of due process, not a fair trial, etc., and he'd entered a guilty plea. Now, he didn't think he should serve any time at all.

The hate-crimes case was haunted—as so many cases are these days—by race. It reminded me of a case I'd had twenty years before when I was practicing criminal law. I referred to it briefly earlier in this book. The incident took place at a high school on the Southside. A white kid stabbed and killed a black kid. Someone had told the white kid's mother to come to see me for help. Her husband had died and this boy was her only son. He was either in the eleventh or twelfth grade. He got out of school one day, and four or five black kids approached him and demanded that he give them his money. They knew he worked after school. He told them he couldn't give them his money because he worked too hard for it and he needed it to help his mother.

They started beating on him. He had a knife in his pickup truck and a gun in the gun rack in the rear window. He got the knife and killed one of the boys when he stabbed him in the throat. My approach was that this was self-defense. I told the jury not to get hung up on race, that this was not a race issue. Those kids were committing armed robbery. The issue was right and wrong. You can't go around just robbing people, and my client had a right to defend himself. I made a motion for a directed verdict, which was unusual in a case like that, but the judge granted it. The judge asked me afterward why I had taken the case.

I said: "Judge, my first year of law school was at Howard University. Howard is a place of causes. Like I tell people all the time, 'suppose all the white lawyers who represented us during the civil rights movement took the position that they weren't going to represent us because we were Afro-American?' That's the same issue involved in this case. I represented him, even though I got criticized for it, because the cause was right. He was innocent."

It made me proud that I could use my training, my intelligence, and my skills to keep the judicial system from making a mistake. There's no higher calling.

I just wish that more of the cases that come before the court today held the same sense of pride for me. As I've settled into this position and gained more perspective on what it means to sit where I sit, I'm distressed by so much of what I see. So many young people, black and white—but particularly African Americans— come through the system on drugs, especially crack cocaine. There is so much violence, senseless violence. That's largely what I meant earlier when I said the job of helping young people succeed is such a serious challenge. So many of our black youngsters today seem lost. Their conduct is scary. Their education and training are lacking, as is any motivation or sense of purpose. I see it every day. Young men come with little or no regard for human life, with little or no ambition. More of them come through the courtroom than I care to count. Young women come also, who can hardly read or write, and who don't fully understand what's going on in their lives, or in the courtroom.

A young lady I date from time to time called me recently and said she had stopped at a fish market called Nikki's near the corner of Northside Drive and Whitehall Street. She said a young girl, sixteen or seventeen years old, was standing outside the store talking on a cell phone. The girl was telling someone that Nikki's was packed, but that she didn't go in anyway because she had just come to that location to smoke crack cocaine. This teen was in a public place talking about smoking crack, and she didn't care who heard her. My friend shook her head in sadness.

A few months ago, I presided over a case in which a twenty-two-year-old black art student got together with three of his friends; they pooled their money, and the art student went to buy $2,000 worth of marijuana. The dealer ripped off the student and took the money. When the young man went back to his "friends," they told him that either he was going to get their money back that night or he was going to die.

The testimony at trial was that the young man told them he could come up with $400 that night, and on Friday when he was paid, he would give them his whole paycheck. He tried to get the rest of the money from his mother. They called the young man's mother in Florida and told her that her son had to come up with $2,000 that night, or he would die.

The mother was screaming over the telephone, begging them not to kill her son. She told them that it was Sunday—no banks were open—that she would get the money and drive to Georgia with it the next morning. She also told them to call the young man's uncle in DeKalb County, which they did. The uncle told them that if they waited until the next day, he would give them $5,000.

One of the guys took charge of the situation and told the uncle that he wasn't going to go for their "bullshit." He shot the art student four times in the head. The shooter was sixteen or seventeen years old. I sentenced him to life in prison.

The mother of one of the others accused was listening to testimony during the trial and asked that we stop the trial. She spoke to her son out of the presence of the jury. She told him that he was just as guilty as the one who pulled the trigger. She told him to plead guilty; he did, and I sentenced him to life.

The third kid's situation made me furious. The DA had granted him immunity and he was getting off scot-free for testifying against the others. When it was time for him to get on the witness stand and testify truthfully, he lied. Because some of his testimony was proven to be untrue, he lost his immunity. He received some credit for bringing his friends to justice, but he was sentenced to twenty years.

Cases like that affect me tremendously because I'm a parent, too. One of my kids or grandchildren could be the victim or one of the killers, except for the grace of God.

Sometimes, the things I see and hear and the things I must do are incredibly difficult. But if I've got to put somebody in jail, I'll do it. Yet, I'm always looking for some mitigating circumstances to help balance things off. In the end, though, I don't lose sleep at night.

But it does make me pause.

As I sit here now, I can't help but wonder what has happened to us, to black people. What has happened to our younger generation? There is so much violence. Life is so cheap. We've lost our standards. Where are the young Constance Baker Motleys, the young Thurgood Marshalls, the young Donald Hollowells, the young Lonnie Kings? Where are the morals?

That's why I'm still at it, still working in my community, still trying to tutor young people, trying to encourage them.

Sometimes, it does get to be too much. I have to take vacations to clear my mind. I plan my calendar on a yearly basis and try to carve out three weeks over the year during which I can travel. I like to go out to Sante Fe, New Mexico. They have the big Native American market out there and a friend and I go for a week, eat southwest food, browse, walk, and take in the culture of the city.

Other times, I like to go down to St. Simons Island and relax close to the water. The other day, right here in the city, my four-year-old granddaughter and I went swimming. I think I enjoyed it more than she did. And I love to cook. You have to release that stress, or you'll go crazy.

I am well into my sixties now, and I've been doing a lot of looking back over my life. What is a life, after all? It is more than just a litany of accomplishments or recollections on trials overcome. It is about meaning and principles and helping others to make your specific community, in a specific time, a better place to live. It is about giving, repaying, and trying to leave things better than you found them. I have been blessed in more ways than I can count. By serving others, serving in public life, I have enriched myself in innumerable ways. I've gotten to travel to places I probably never would have seen if I hadn't chosen government service. I've been to France, Germany, Portugal, Spain, Switzerland, England, the Netherlands, Tanzania, the Sudan, Austria, Morocco, Korea, Taiwan, Puerto Rico, the Dominican Republic, Aruba, and Uganda—not to mention many, many places in this country.

My life has been rich and, I hope, useful. More than anything, though, I hope young people will look at it and see themselves. They might see where I came from and how far I've gone. They might look at me and know that they, too, can rise above their current stations in life, above other people's low expectations. Even above their own self doubts.

And that will make all the difference. For me—and for them.

Acknowledgments

It is impossible for me to thank everyone who has traveled with me on my journey, but I say a special thanks to those who encouraged me and assisted in making this autobiography a reality.

My personal thanks to Ralph Redding, who taught me as a boy how to fend for myself; my mentor, the late K. C. Marks, who gave me my first paper route in my old neighborhood; my brother, Joseph Arrington, who "preached" the value of a formal education; the late Lois Wright, my fifth-grade teacher at English Avenue Elementary School; and Evangeline Winkfield, who taught me in the sixth grade at A. F. Herndon Elementary School. I would like to thank my former high school coach, Raymond "Tweet" Williams, who secured an athletic scholarship for me to attend Clark College, and the late L. S. Epps, my college football coach, who demanded the very best from his athletes and taught us never to give up.

A special thanks to my former classmate and personal friend, Dr. Delores Aldridge, and the late Dr. Hamilton E. Holmes, a lifetime friend. The two of them played a major role in my success in undergraduate school.

I want to thank Lonnie King, who urged me to run for public office here in Atlanta in the early 60s. Also, I would like to thank my former classmate, the late Ben Brown, whom I thought was a classic student leader—bold, creative, articulate—and who urged me to pursue my law degree at Howard University.

Also, I thank Chet Fuller, who served as a consultant in writing this book; Dr. Regina Johnson; Gwendolyn Mayfield; A. Randy Eaddy; Don Plummer, Reginald Williams; Lowell Dickerson; Jeffrey Riddle; Cathy Lyon; David Getachew-Smith; Mildred Williams; Judith Hanson; Harriett Thomas; the late Gary Holmes; Cathy Joyce; Gregory Coleman; Dr. Aruby Odom-White; Hill Jefferies; Henry R. Bauer, Jr.; S. Richard Rubin; and S. Richard Rubin, my former law partner. It was with their encouragement that I forged ahead and tried to capture my life growing up in Atlanta—a city I love dearly.

A special thanks to the late Ben F. Johnson II, who admitted both US District Court Judge Clarence Cooper and me to Emory University Law School.

Thank you to all of the African-American educators who accepted the responsibility of teaching me and others in the Atlanta Public School System. These gifted individuals came armed with knowledge, few resources, and a total commitment for their students to succeed.

Thank you, too, for your support along the way.

Cordially,

Marvin

Index

Index

Index